T0208511

Praise for *Red Parrot, Wooden leg*

'It was a great pleasure to read. In finishing the novel, I felt tremendous sadness – the last section is marvellous. What is done so well in the book is the creation of atmosphere – whether political intimidation, the ambiguous threats of magic, or just erotic possibilities. The bizarre, semi-surreal outrageous scenes are quite brilliant, and the spirit of amazing mischief is irresistible. The disturbing links with the political violence haunts the novel.'

Adam Phillips

'A highly original, often comical *Bildungsroman*. The Beat writers of the period – Kerouac, Ginsberg, Henry Miller – are his models. Yet so extraordinary is the blend of European, African and native Indian cultures in Brazil, that the experiences of the characters often have the hallucinatory quality characteristic of Latin American magical realism. The book's great strength lies in the way it explores the place of love and friendship, on the one hand, and beliefs and ideas on the other, in young lives that are at the mercy of politics, history, superstition, and passion.'

Jill Kitson

'What an extraordinary adventure! I read this book with nostalgia, with recognition, grateful that somebody else also remembered. We are all witnesses of witnesses.'

Alberto Manguel

'A beautifully written, highly engaging novel. The dialogue is sparing and highly nuanced. I was particularly taken by the way in which the atmosphere of the time is a living character in the book.'

Tom Ogden

'[The book] explores coming of age. Daniel grew up in Buenos Aires and is now living in Rio de Janeiro, his hedonistic lifestyle... in stark contrast to the repression that pervaded South America in the Sixties: Daniel is carefree, writing poetry and living in a miniature commune with his girlfriend, a prostitute he meets in a bar. But letters from home bring him back in touch with a reality he's trying to forget. These letters, written by his friend Damian, are the highlights of the book, sharp and frightening insights into the rising political tensions in Argentina...'

The Observer

'Argentinian-born Gregorio Kohon is a renowned psychoanalyst and a poet, so you would be forgiven for not expecting his debut novel to have a light touch. This, however, has just that: a coming-of-age tale, it is as lusty and spirited as it is thoughtful.'

The Financial Times

'...this is a diary in the style of the Beats, with homage to Kerouac, Ginsberg and Miller. It extends its reach to Brazil in the throes of the new sounds of bossa nova and tropicalia. The encounter between the bourgeois porteños of Buenos Aires and the alternative lifestyle cariocas of Rio lends the book a character as original as that of the lame parrot.'

The Independent

'Its main protagonist is a poet drawing on both his Jewish roots and Brazilian folklore...'

The Jewish Chronicle

'A short story about a man venturing into the jungle became a novel exploring Rio de Janeiro's exotic nightlife. The novel was first published in Spanish and short-listed for a prestigious literary prize.'

Ham&High

'The novel recreates the oppressive atmosphere of Ongania's government, it evokes its acts of cruel repression, and it remembers the hidden presence of torture and persecution.'

Clarín

'The book is so rich and exotic. I liked the feeling of a relishing of life –even a relishing of the sadness… a liberating book to read.'

Nell Dunn

'This wonderful book is a great achievement. The beginning has such a great "feel", so internally effervescent that it is irresistible. But the tone darkens after the high-spirited opening pages, and the reader gets a real sense of the fear and claustrophobia of living in Brazil or Argentina in the 60s and 70s. The horror of the oppressors is beautifully rendered, and the whole thing moves toward a gorgeous ending. Kind of a soft landing, a farewell kiss of an ending.'

Peter Straub

'A moving story, centred around the theme of literary creativity…'

Última Hora

'In his psychoanalytic books, Kohon has amply demonstrated what a good writer he is. But this is not just the work of a psychoanalyst who happens to write well. This is an original first novel of an accomplished poet: erotic, humorous, exotic and sensuous. It describes the adventures of two young writers, set in the midst of political repression, anti-Semitism and violence during the Latin American dictatorships of Brazil and Argentina in the 60s. Kohon's text might be deceptively read as personal reminiscences. In fact, this is one of the many achievements of this wonderful piece of fiction. A writer of great talent and promise.'

Rosie Scott

'This entertaining and moving novel subtly explores the complex relationship between creativity, institutionalised repression, and the challenge of growing up. What had started as an act of freedom and pleasure, the history of a trip through strange territories, ends up as a true Bildungsroman.'

Jason Wilson

'In a novel which is a useful reminder that the serpent's egg was already being hatched in the sixties before the Proceso (under the dictatorship of Videla's junta in the seventies), Gregorio Kohon, with a deft hand, paints a colourful portrait of a lost generation – their broken dreams somehow symbolised by the title.'

The Buenos Aires Herald

RED PARROT, WOODEN LEG

RED PARROT, WOODEN LEG

by Gregorio Kohon

Routledge
Taylor & Francis Group
LONDON AND NEW YORK

First published 2007 by Karnac Books Ltd.

This paperback edition published in 2008.

Published 2018 by Routledge
2 Park Square, Milton Park, Abingdon, Oxon OX14 4RN
711 Third Avenue, New York, NY 10017, USA

Routledge is an imprint of the Taylor & Francis Group, an informa business

British Library Cataloguing in Publication Data

A C.I.P. for this book is available from the British Library

ISBN-13: 9781855756939 (pbk)

Designed, and produced by HL Studios, Long Hanborough, Oxford

BY THE SAME AUTHOR

POETRY (in Spanish)

Puntos de Partida

Ebrio Sale el Sol

Odetta en Babilonia y el Rápido a Canadá

El Estilo del Deseo

FICTION (in Spanish)

Papagayo Rojo, Pata de Palo

PSYCHOANALYSIS

The British School of Psychoanalysis – The Independent Tradition
(Editor)

The Dead Mother- The Work of André Green (Editor)

No Lost Certainties to be Recovered

Love and its Vicissitudes (co-authored with André Green)

To Antonio Dal Masetto

CONTENTS

About the Author   xvii

Chapter 1 - 1966   1

    Part I   3

    Part II   79

    Part III   145

    Part IV   173

Chapter 2 - 1971   211

Chapter 3 - 1986   215

Acknowledgements   219

A Note on Translation   220

... true as only fiction can be.

Emmanuel Lévinas

About the Author

Gregorio Kohon was born in Buenos Aires and qualified as a clinical psychologist at the Universidad de La Plata. He moved to England to study and work with R.D.Laing and the anti-psychiatry movement. Later, he trained as a psychoanalyst with the British Psychoanalytical Society, qualifying as an Associate Member in 1979, and as a Training Analyst in 1999. He and his family lived in Australia from 1988 to 1994. He directed the Brisbane Centre for Psychoanalytic Studies, which he co-founded with Valli, his wife. Kohon has written and edited four psychoanalytic books. He is also a poet and has published three books of poems as well as being included in many anthologies of Argentinian poetry. His next collection of poems, *El Estilo del Deseo*, will be published by Grupo Editorial Latinoamericano. The manuscript of his novel *Papagayo Rojo, Pata de Palo* was a finalist in the 2001 Fernando Lara Prize, Editorial Planeta, Barcelona. He lives in London.

1966

PART I

1

Cockroaches. Those indestructible creatures.

They had defeated time, the Ice Age, powerful poisons and professional hunters. The unconquerable bastards. Rio de Janeiro was full of them.

He quickly learned to love the city, its avenues running parallel to the sea, the mountains, the way people smiled, the way they walked. And those women: their hips set the world on fire.

A poet and friend who worked for the Brazilian Cultural Attaché had helped him get on a military flight that carried the artists, the diplomatic parcels, the poor, and the deportees. There were no seats on the plane; instead, people perched like parachutists on two rows of metal benches set along its length. The contraption rattled and shook; the cold seeping through the cracks in the walls was unbearable. He and a black woman, holding a small child on her lap, were the only passengers. Sitting opposite him, she seemed frightened and might have been praying. He smiled. The woman, with an absent look in her eyes, didn't respond. This was his first trip on a plane. Without a God to protect him, Daniel not only felt afraid but forsaken.

He rented a room in a flat near the sea, in Copacabana. It had a bed which was too short, a table with a broken lamp, an old wardrobe, and it smelt of damp. There was just enough space to open the door. The landlady was a woman in her thirties who lived in the flat with her adolescent daughter; they took in laundry for a living. In order to get to his room, he had to make his way through a patio full of sheets, underwear, jeans, T-shirts, socks and towels. As they worked, the mother and daughter sang romantic songs:

Good-bye, my love,
The sea is waiting for me…

They giggled, talked about him and teased him. They made him feel wanted.

At night, life changed. The repugnant visitors with their flattened oval bodies swarmed through his dreams. Cockroaches were everywhere. Falling asleep, he would feel their antennae tickling his skin under the sheet, hear their legs scratching against the newspapers on the floor. He lay in bed every night, listening, tensely anticipating their inevitable visits, inventing strategies to resist the invasion. He decided not to give in. He would train himself to catch the bastards, convinced that he could win. Damned *blattella germanica*.

Every night he lit a couple of candles, and awaited their arrival. Books, tennis balls, old pieces of bread, and shoes weren't very effective. A small but firm pillow was his best weapon: it stunned the monsters enough to make them easy prey. His nightly catch started with five specimens; the more he developed his technique, the more cockroaches he caught. One exceptional night he scored thirty-six. He placed each night's catch in small opaque plastic bags and, while the two women were asleep, stored them at the back of the landlady's freezer, behind the packages of meat. The next night he would place a new bag of cockroaches in the freezer, throwing away the frozen ones, now definitely dead.

This trip to Rio was meant to be a short jaunt but, unable to decide what to do with his life, he simply didn't show up for the return flight. Only a few weeks earlier, the publication of his first book of poems in Buenos Aires had been celebrated with a party at an art gallery in calle Florida; to the raucous jamming of local rock bands, people danced till dawn. It had ended in a stampede provoked by two drunken policemen. The following day the headlines of a morning paper lied: "COMMUNIST WRITER'S PARTY ENDS IN SHOOT-OUT". That morning, his friend Damián helped him hide politically sensitive books and papers. He stayed in different places for a while until the whole business blew over. Meanwhile, the book sold out.

Soon after his arrival in Rio, he recited his poetry at the Catholic University, talked on the radio, was interviewed on television and even wrote theatre reviews for a literary magazine. Anything was possible: Rio was there for the taking. And he had been lucky: through friends and literary contacts, he was offered a grant by the Brazilian government for foreign artists and writers. One of those contradictions of Latin American governments: on the one hand, repression; on the other, support for literature and the arts. Given the exchange rate, four hundred dollars amounted to a small fortune. He immediately rang Luigi and invited him to join him.

Luigi had already made up his mind to do so, even before hearing about the grant. He gave notice to his employers, said goodbye to his two girlfriends (Monday, Wednesday and Friday, it was Iris; Tuesday, Thursday and Sunday, Hortensia; Saturday, religiously free). On the plane, Luigi met the leader of an obscure sect of spiritualists; they disembarked drunk, embracing each other while weaving across the landing strip. Daniel watched them from a distance: the two men embraced again, talked some more, shook hands and finally went their separate ways.

Luigi had brought a letter from Daniel's parents, small presents from his two sisters, and lots of cigarettes – black tobacco, their favourite. The spiritualist leader had offered him the name and address of someone who might put them up for free. Given Daniel's secret war against the *germánicas*, he readily agreed to accompany Luigi and try the place out.

The address was near the University cafeteria, which the students called *o calabozo* – the jail. They strolled down Avenida Presidente Vargas, past the small shops selling clothes and cheap jewellery, the noisy square, the police station. Daniel wanted to know the latest news in Argentina. Meanwhile, Luigi bombarded him with questions. Where was he living? Had he met any Brazilian women? Had he shagged any? What were the beaches like?

A young, tall, skinny black man opened the door. "Who are you?"he said, looking them over. "How did you get in? The front door is locked at all times."

"It wasn't."Luigi responded, handing over the spiritualist's letter of introduction. The man had a long, thin, white animal bone hanging from his right ear, an amulet against the evil eye. From his left ear hung a small and delicate pendant: a wooden thumb inserted between the first and second fingers of a clenched fist. After reading the letter somewhat disdainfully, the man invited them in.

The room was large and dark. There were no pictures on the walls and a curtain of cheap blue velvet hid the window. On one side of the room was a round table, covered by a plastic cloth patterned in big red and white flowers. The place needed cleaning and was starved of fresh air. Two black men sat at the table manicuring their nails. The man who had opened the door, now more relaxed, took charge of the introductions.

"I'm Socrates. These are my friends Amadeu and Fulvio, our *pommes de terre en robe de chambre.*"

"Potatoes in dressing gowns?" Was it a pun, or some private joke?

"*Mais oui, messieurs*, we *are* hot,"added Fulvio. The three smiled at one another suggestively. Amadeu, the ugly one, asked whether the visitors were spiritualists. Luigi said they were writers, they just wanted a room. For free. After another exchange of significant looks, Socrates asked:

"Do you believe in spirits?"No time for them to reply. "Nothing is more important in life, the spirit is our most essential part; it is what makes relations possible between the living and the dead. Without spirit, life has no meaning."

"The spirit is the only thing that survives our bodies once we die, and we all die, sooner or later,"added Fulvio. "The spirit, once disembodied, lives forever in another world."

"Yes!"the others agreed.

Maybe life with the *germánicas* was not that bad after all.

"Nobody in their right mind could deny the existence of immaterial reality,"said Luigi. They hadn't been invited to sit down yet. "Nevertheless,"he continued, "I'm opposed to spiritualism. I support Giovanni Gentile, for whom the pure activity of self-consciousness is the sole reality."

The three Brazilians looked lost and tried to recover. According to Socrates, evidence of materialisation went back a long way, to Biblical times: "The spirit of the prophet Samuel appeared to Saul while the King was visiting the witch of Endor. Doesn't that have any meaning for you? It's in the Old Testament!'

"So? Poor King Saul was completely out of his mind,"Luigi argued, "so scared of the coming battle that he lost his marbles. Anyway, from Spinoza we know that there is nothing in the Bible that says the soul is immortal."

Daniel felt it was time to make a move: he stepped forward and grabbed two chairs, positioning them in front of Socrates. They sat down and remained silent. After a while, they were offered tea and Socrates disappeared into the kitchen; Fulvio and Amadeo went back to their manicures. Luigi tore open another packet of cigarettes. Then, they all drank sweetened iced tea with lemon, and ate coconut biscuits and *pupunha*, a fruit from the Amazon. Inevitably, they ended up talking about soccer. Pelé.

Garrincha. No more spiritual things. A while later, Daniel asked: "What about the room, then?"

"You can move in tonight, if you wish,"said Socrates.

In the streets, people from offices and shops nearby were out for lunch. The heat was stifling. For some, to interrupt their work was just an excuse to have another coffee, another beer in the bars. People talked and shouted and seemed to argue fanatically just about everything, from soccer to politics.

"Where did you get all that shit about the spirit?"

"When I was younger, I was overwhelmed: permanent erections, dirty thoughts, wet dreams every night. Once I tried to screw my sister, who was two years older than me. I couldn't stop masturbating, I was losing my mind, sex was such a problem. I thought that priesthood was the way to go."

"And then, what happened?'

"Not much. Things didn't work out for me. I left the seminary after a couple of years."

They got to a small dingy beach in the centre of town.

"Is that the Sugar Loaf?"asked Luigi, pointing.

There was a cable car that took people to the top of the mountain. "The view of the city is something else,"Daniel told him.

They sat on the sand. A gentle breeze had started to blow. This dirty beach wasn't the best place to introduce Luigi to the *carioca* sea, but Daniel couldn't be bothered to go any further.

Luigi was four years older. He had already published several short stories in literary magazines. The son of Italian immigrants, poor peasants from the mountains of Catanzaro, in Calabria, he was short and stocky; his small hands, hardened by the days he had spent as a carpenter on building sites, were always holding a cigarette. Luigi's father – like so many Italian immigrants – had joined the anarchist movement as soon as he arrived in Buenos Aires. It was the time of the Sacco and Vanzetti scandal in the USA, of home-made bombs used against the police, of writing for the weekly *Vita Libertaria*. While his father spent most of his time organising strikes, the family lived on his mother's meagre income from her job as a maid for wealthy families.

Luigi's clear blue eyes shone out of his dark complexion. Shy and guarded at first, his caustic humour soon broke through; then he became talkative, funny and eloquent, an instant hit with women. At the beginning, Daniel found Luigi's silences difficult to take. He came from a large, loud and extrovert family: more than talking, they barked and growled at each other. All this vocal activity was performed in Yiddish, it always sounded contentious.

Luigi pulled out a bottle of vodka from his backpack. "My mother gave it to me at the airport, she thought we would need it. It was a present from her Polish neighbour, who I suspect is in love with her."

"How old is your mother?"

"Fifty-two, she dresses all in black like a traditional Mediterranean widow. She's still very attractive, a lot of men chase after her."

The liquid, a brownish colour, wasn't the normal kind of vodka. The label said *For Export*. "Sixty fucking proof! This will kill us."The first sip didn't sit well on their empty stomachs; by the fourth, they couldn't have cared less.

"This vodka is poison, we can't go on drinking it."Luigi happily proceeded to empty the rest of the liquid in the sand. He *was* drunk.

"You know, in our last encounter,"Daniel said, also definitely drunk, "she punched through a window and made a mess of her right arm, it was horrible."

"Who?"

"Lola. I don't know how many stitches she had to have, she fucked up one of her tendons."

"Forget Lola, man, that's finished, *kaput!* No room for melancholy today."

Luigi got a pen out of his pocket and wrote a note on a piece of paper. It read: "I am so far away, so alone, so high". He rolled it up and pushed it inside the bottle. He found a cork in the sand, and stopped up the bottle. He raced towards the sea and hurled the bottle with all his might; the few people on the beach ignored him. They heard the soft splash at some distance. Luigi came back and sat down again. "I hope it'll get to Paris."

"To Cortázar!"Daniel added with enthusiasm. And then, "Do you think we should move to the House of Spiritualism? We have some money, we can rent somewhere else."

Luigi looked serious and remained silent. Daniel couldn't understand what he had said wrong.

"We discovered that it was the priest. My mother wants to kill him…"

Daniel instantly understood. Luigi's sister had given birth to a baby boy just before Daniel left the country.

"Is *he* the father of the baby?"

"Yes."

Daniel exploded in laughter. He had to get up so he wouldn't choke. He laughed until his stomach and jaw started to ache.

"You son of a bitch, you motherfucking asshole, you ignorant bastard."And finally, "You fucking dirty Jew…"Luigi knew *that* would stop him.

Daniel delivered a punch to Luigi's shoulder, who responded with a right cross to Daniel's head. They locked in a wrestler's clinch. It was for real, but it didn't last long.

"I think we're even,"Daniel said.

"I think you're mad,"Luigi answered.

Daniel began to recite:

> *In the middle of the road I found a stone.*
> *I will never forget that event. . .*

It didn't seem possible but this irreverent piece of writing had set off a revolution in Brazilian poetry. Maybe, after all, there was justice in the world.

They decided to collect Daniel's belongings and move into the spiritualists' flat. Through the small windows of the small bus the different *carioca* beaches whizzed past them, one more beautiful than the other. When the *lotaçaô* reached Copacabana, the place was in high gear: old ladies walking their dogs, middle-aged men jogging, youngsters cooling themselves in the water, prostitutes buying their groceries. When Luigi saw a young woman wearing a bikini, he shouted at her, still happy on vodka, "*Cara, ti amo, chè bella sei, bellíssima!*"

The flat was on the second floor. Luigi and Daniel raced up the stairs to the entrance, just as the owner's daughter was taking out the rubbish. She shouted, "Ma! Ma! He's here! He's here!'

As they crossed the threshold, they came face to face with the landlady. "You brute, you dirty animal! I reported you to the police!"she yelled at him.

It took him a few seconds to remember the frozen cockroaches, neatly stacked at the back of the freezer. He ran to his room while she continued to complain loudly to Luigi, who knew nothing about the cockroaches and was stunned by her fury. Daniel threw all his clothes into a suitcase, slipped his few books into a plastic bag, hurriedly retrieved his toothbrush and toothpaste from the bathroom, and left with Luigi trailing behind him. From the landing, he shouted, "And I am going to report you to the Health Department, you cow."

As they reached the street, he explained to Luigi about the *germánicas*.

"Oh, I thought that you had seduced her daughter and that she was jealous. . ."

When they got to the spiritualists' place, Socrates opened the door. He seemed genuinely glad to see them. He was wearing a pair of orange soccer shorts, very tight and shiny, and a T-shirt with the head of Carmen Miranda, fruit and all, printed on the back. His eyes were made up in heavy dark blue, he had red lipstick on. He bent down to help them with the bags, making sure he showed his small, almost perfectly rounded breasts. No trace of the previous belligerence.

Socrates showed them to their bedroom which was spacious and quite dark, despite its large windows. It was furnished with a sofa covered in fake leopard skin, a huge old wardrobe with a mirror and a double bed.

"Is this OK?"Socrates called from the corridor. "The bathroom is next door. It's the only one and we all share it."

"Well, the room is big enough, and it's free,"Daniel said to Luigi, closing the door. "No complaints."They unpacked, Daniel placing his few books on the windowsill and Luigi adding his own collection: Salvatore Quasimodo, Jorge Amado, Raúl González Tuñón, Roberto Arlt, Cesare Pavese.

"We even have a library of essential authors now, not bad, *eh?*"Luigi joked.

"I'm dead tired,"said Daniel.

Having arranged the pillows, one at each end, they lay down, had a cigarette, and fell asleep.

When he woke up, the rich smell of fried plantain invaded the room. It was about seven in the evening and the nap had revived him. As he headed for the shower, he could hear Luigi's voice coming from another room. The tiles around the tub, once white, were now yellowish; the reflection of the light-bulb hanging from the ceiling gave the bathroom the surreal feel of a movie set.

After drying himself and putting on clean clothes, he went to the kitchen where he found Luigi sitting in a corner. While they cooked dinner, the three black men were hotly criticising the government. They wanted the military dictator in power to implement more efficient economic policies.

"We needed a tough guy,"Fulvio asserted, "someone with balls. That's why we support the new government; our ex-President, *Jango* Goulart, allowed too much political freedom. Democracy is not good for us. It's very clear, we needed a military coup to stop the communists."

"You don't understand this country, we're not civilised, like Argentina,"Socrates pointed out.

Poor and unemployed, the transvestites must have been earning a living by doing odd jobs, perhaps even turning the occasional trick, yet they were right-wing to the core. "Ché Guevara, there's no hope", Daniel thought.

The three transvestites played host, setting the table and lighting candles all around the living room. Amadeu offered Daniel a *caipirinha*, prepared with great devotion. "The best I've tried so far,"Daniel complimented him. He had to do a lot of drinking to catch up with the others.

The Brazilians looked stunning, all dressed up for the evening in tight skinny trousers and garishly flowered satin shirts – their best finery. Luigi and Daniel were invited to sit at the table. Fulvio had cooked *caruru*, a dish made with a *garoupa* fish, okra, shrimps and *malagueta* pepper. "My mother taught me to cook,"Fulvio volunteered. "She used to dress me like a girl when my father wasn't around; I had to pretend to be her little daughter. It was so much fun, I never felt so loved...'

"What about your lawyer friend, babe?"Socrates intervened wickedly, making sure that the dignified atmosphere wouldn't turn solemn. `He loved you too,"Socrates added. Everybody burst out laughing.

"That was lust,"Fulvio responded, drawing out the vowels and pursing his lips, simulating an exaggerated kiss. "Pure and unadulterated lust."

"He was something else, wasn't he? So good looking!"Amadeu intervened.

"He was mad, he wanted to marry me. One day he took me to meet his parents, a rich family from Manaus, imagine, my black Saint Christopher! We all went to the opera at the Teatro Amazonas, and saw *Manon Lescaut*; I cried so much that his parents decided I was mentally unbalanced. They objected to us staying together. I wore an outrageously low-cut dress that night and my future father-in-law couldn't stop looking at my tits!"

After dinner, Socrates brought out some coffee. In the wake of all those *caipirinhas* and the *caruru*, they had calmed down. Time for confessions.

Socrates came from the country near the city of Cuiaba, the starting point for exploring *el Pantanal*. He was born at the beginning of July, on the day of the *Festa de Sâo Benedito* -a popular celebration. Socrates believed for many years that everybody in town was celebrating his birth: he had been born under a lucky star. He was baptised at the Chapel of Saint Benedict, and this had been followed by an *umbanda* ceremony, with African dances and traditional food. When the festivities were over, Socrates became ill. They feared for his life; the family doctor could do nothing to stop his fever. He even had a couple of convulsions that sent his parents into a panic. Socrates' grandmother, who had not intervened until then, suggested calling an old medicine man, the *pajé* of the Bororo Indians of the Pantanal.

The *pajé*, Socrates' father, and Socrates were locked in a hut for thirty-six hours, during which time the medicine man chanted, danced, killed a couple of chickens and lit several fires. After all the ceremonies were completed, he declared the infant cured. Years later, his father explained to Socrates that – according to the *pajé* – he had been the reincarnation of a male transvestite from the Guiacuru tribe, a nomadic group of Indians that used to take male transvestites with them on long journeys, leaving their women behind. The medicine man had given Socrates a new name during the ceremony, Carmela. According to his father (who had called him Carmela all his life), this had saved him. Nevertheless, for the rest of the family he had remained Socrates.

In order to bolster their meagre budget, his parents took in paying guests. When Socrates was ten, a young Frenchman with a long moustache and a deep voice stayed at the house, on and off, for several months. He announced he was a zoologist, but was secretly running one of the most profitable rackets in the Pantanal. Using small aeroplanes, he smuggled all sorts of animals across the nearby borders of Bolivia and Paraguay: giant anteaters, jaguars, anacondas and iguanas, black howler monkeys and hyacinth macaws, toucans, thorn birds, herons and woodpeckers, rare fish from the rivers and, above all, jacares - the skin of which was used to make handbags and shoes.

To avoid being caught, the Frenchman kept moving around the Pantanal from one place to another, living in people's houses, bribing the local police and rangers with money and watered-down French brandy. He specially favoured Socrates' place for its proximity to the whorehouse. He had taken Socrates under his wing, and had taught him a few French words: *la bouche, le soleil, le paysage*. He also showed the boy *La Vie privée de Marie-Antoinette*, a book with erotic illustrations, including the Queen's graceful encounters with her ladies-in-waiting. During the lazy afternoons of the rainy season, Socrates would look at the pictures for hours on end; the French smuggler translated the captions, explained the text, and probably added his own invented stories.

In this way, Socrates became obsessed with Marie-Antoinette: he started making little drawings of her face and painted pictures of an imaginary Petit Trianon, her rustic retreat. He wanted to know everything about Versailles, the sacking of the Tuileries, the French Revolution. The Frenchman told him about Louis XVI's impotence, and how Marie-Antoinette had then turned her sexual interest towards women. He described her friendships with the delicate Princesse de Lamballe and the attractive Comtesse de Polignac, her affairs with Lucie Dillon and Mme Balbi. Socrates took these stories in with the same fascination with which other children listened to Little Red Riding Hood.

One element made a particular impression on him: how the Princess de Lamballe had been mutilated and murdered, how the drunken mob carried her head on a pike to where Marie-Antoinette was imprisoned, how they forced her to kiss the lips of her former lover. "It was the most wonderfully romantic love story ever. I felt very close to Marie-Antoinette, and often dreamt of being in that prison, living out the last days of her life. Later on, in my adolescence, I won several Carnival prizes dressed up as her."

At the same time, he also started having frequent hypnotic trances, with visions and hallucinations and mystical raptures, at the end of which Socrates seemed to be trying to kill himself – usually choking himself by forcing his tongue down his throat. His parents were convinced he wanted to die, so he could reincarnate as a woman. They took him to a spiritualist healer, who declared that the Bororo medicine man had been wrong, that he had made a mistake in his interpretation of the situation, and proceeded to rename him Socrates again. He felt reborn; predictably, he became part of the healer's church and moved to Rio.

"*Voilá! C'est tout!*"Socrates said.

After a long and thoughtful silence, Luigi started to talk to Socrates, while Fulvio and Amadeu whispered to each other softly. Daniel, left on his own in a corner, was happy to be sitting there, contemplating the others, thinking, "Is Socrates falling in love with Luigi?" He was happy to have moved. It hadn't been that bad at the flat (except for the *germánicas*) but living in Copacabana had made him feel like a tourist. He shared the Brazilian passion for football and anarchic respect for poetry, the arts, architecture, music, dance. The mixture suited him just fine. He didn't want to go on feeling like a foreigner.

They all washed up, wiped the table, and Amadeo insisted on sweeping and mopping the kitchen floor. "If not, the cockroaches will have a feast,"he said.

Daniel suggested going to Lapa, a district he had not yet dared to visit. "If what you guys want are women, you don't have to go that far,"Fulvio said.

"Let them go, let them go,"joked Amadeo. "We might not be able to offer what they need."

"I was told it isn't only a red light district,"protested Daniel.

"Of course there are other things…"Amadeo teased them.

"Yes, poverty!"cried Fulvio.

"Go on, you should visit it, Lapa's worth seeing,"said Socrates. It was obvious: the transvestites would have been open to suggestions but they weren't pushing it; they let them go.

Fulvio produced a bottle of rose petal perfume, and dabbed a bit behind their ears: "This way, you'll be well received."

Lapa was within walking distance. Luigi broke the silence as they walked along, "I felt strange halfway through dinner."

"I thought you were having a good time."

"When Socrates passed me the sauce, he touched my hand, I don't know, I couldn't see him as a man. They look and feel like women, those eyes, those lips, the breasts they have. Was that happening to you too? I thought he might have been trying to seduce me."

"Brazilian transvestites are displacing the prostitutes in the Bois de Boulogne, so you wouldn't be alone."

"Would you…?"

"Forget it, man, maybe you just drank too much. And almost as an afterthought, he added, "We *have* to find some birds."

It didn't take them long to reach Lapa, near the terminus of the tram that went to el morro de Santa Teresa. Daniel soon understood why he had been repeatedly warned about the dangers of Lapa. The streets were full of prostitutes, hustlers, beggars. Shouts. Fights. Loud music came from restaurants, bars, clubs. In the midst of the chaos, Luigi and Daniel walked down the street with a mixture of arrogant assurance and apprehension. Farther away from the big avenues, the atmosphere grew more disturbing: children begging, women with babies sleeping in doorways. The poverty and misery became unbearable. What kept them going? They stopped at a few bars, drank *cachaça* and beer, didn't talk much. A girl, perhaps only fifteen, stood in a doorway; she had long, badly bleached hair; a slit up her dress showed her legs. Pregnant, she was waiting for clients.

"Man, where are we?"

"*Siamo arrivati*, it's Hell!"

They reached an area where lots of men were walking up and down the street. The houses were all of a similar colonial design: double front doors, kept open, leading to a small entrance hall with five or six steps going up. On each step, leaning against the wall, a prostitute moved rhythmically as if marking a samba beat with her body; she licked her lips, flicking her tongue in and out of her mouth. The men in the street shouted obscenities and lewd compliments, asking for the price of their services.

"We've got to try it," said Luigi.

"I'll wait for you at the bar on the corner." But even as he said this, Daniel was having second thoughts: *Why not? He's right, you should see what it's like with a whore. If Henry Miller did it, you should too...*

Stupid reasoning.

Daniel chose a woman with cinnamon skin; she must have been in her mid-twenties, curly hair, generous breasts. She took him by the hand as he came up the stairs. At the top, the hall opened onto a rather large patio. There was a row of four bidets set against a green wall, the colour of hope. The patio had a huge vine growing over a trellis, and withered black grapes hung down in bunches. Two women were sitting astride the bidets, washing themselves and laughing. The wiry pimp who ran the place was sitting in a corner, drinking *mate*; he was a mulatto with a pockmarked face and deep creases running from his nostrils down to the edges of his mouth. He wore a white singlet and light blue cotton pyjama trousers. Despite his rather sinister looks, he seemed like a neighbour sitting out on a Sunday morning, his thermos flask of hot water in one hand and a plate of small biscuits on his lap. He chatted away to the women on the bidets and gave change to customers who needed it. From time to time, he picked up grapes that had fallen on the tiles and threw them into a flowerpot in the corner. Along the opposite wall was a series of cubicles separated by wooden partitions. Each small entrance had a curtain made of Indian cotton instead of a proper door. Daniel followed the woman into one of these rooms. Out of the corner of his eye, he saw Luigi go into the one next door.

The cubicle was painted a sugary pink, lit by a lamp with a red bulb. A portrait of a black Virgin Mary holding a baby Jesus was the only decoration on the walls. There was a bed with round pillows, a tiny bedside table with a drawer and a plastic bin in a corner. "*Très romantique!*" the transvestites might have said. The woman undressed very quickly, lay against the pillows, and started to massage her thighs vigorously. He just stood there by the bed, disconcerted, not knowing exactly what to do. He could hear Luigi's voice next door and wished he had waited at the bar on the corner after all. She asked Daniel for the money, which she promptly put away in a small purse strapped to her wrist. Then she undid the buttons of his jeans, pulled down his underpants, took his penis between her hands and started talking to it as if it were a baby: "Come on, little one, grow for me, coochy-coochy-coo." Daniel almost burst out laughing, only the thought of the pimp outside drinking *mate* stopped him.

At that point, when Daniel couldn't imagine anything much happening, against all expectations, the thing was growing big for Mummy! She pulled a condom out of the drawer, opened the packet and deftly unrolled the sheath onto his penis. While doing all this, she didn't stop talking for a second; in fact, she had been having a loud conversation with her colleague next door while he was inside her, pumping hard, trying to convince himself that this was a manly thing to be doing. What he really wanted was protection, comfort, cuddles, security. Daniel needed a wet-nurse, not a whore.

Suddenly, she slapped him for biting one of her nipples: *"Merda!* Are you crazy?"Indignant and furious, she proceeded to tell her friend at full volume what had happened while Daniel came with the pathetic cry of a wounded animal.

It was late, it had started to rain. The few men wandering around were now quiet. Despite the late hour, some young children, undernourished and tired, wearing oversized Salvation Army uniforms, paraded through the streets, singing hymns. Two adult officers in short trousers led the procession, one carrying a wooden box for donations; the other, a tambourine. Following the procession, there was a woman, drunk and almost naked, dragging an enormous dead boa constrictor behind her. From time to time, she would hold the snake by the head and fling it about, trying to hit anyone nearby. She threatened Hell to all sinners and life sentences for the whores.

He went to the bar on the corner where they had agreed to meet. He ordered a beer and a packet of crisps. A man was playing the accordion by the counter; when he heard Daniel's accent, he started singing tangos in an improvised Spanish. Perfect background music for such an occasion.

Soon after, Luigi appeared and he too asked for a beer. "She wanted me to wear a condom. *That* put me off a bit, but … anyway, it was great."

"Just what we needed!"lied Daniel.

2

Soon, almost without noticing it, they fell into a kind of routine. By day, they went sightseeing: the Pâo de Açúcar, the Cristo Redentor, the museums, the Jardim Botânico. On the Corcovado, Luigi insisted on spending quite a while at the top; he seemed moved, not so much by the statue of Christ with his outstretched arms, but by the sheer number of visitors gathered around him. His only comment on the way down was, "They are wasting their time, God doesn't listen."

In Buenos Aires they had never seen such poverty. And yet, Rio had a special rhythm, a contagious buzz; for the *cariocas*, living and enjoying life gained priority over everything else. Luigi and Daniel both seemed to have adapted well; they lived in a state of permanent excitement. *La mufa*, that chronic sullen mood so typical of Buenos Aires, had disappeared.

After each trip to a tourist site, they would collect the mail from the Argentine Consulate. They hardly ever received any letters; it was just part of the daily routine. One day – to his great surprise – Daniel got two, one from Lola and one from his mother. Lola's was very brief:

*Danny, I miss you. I wish I could be there with you. Nobody knows
that alone, at night, one sticks poisoned pins into one's eyes. Lolaila.*

Without the vodka for export in his veins, the letter left him
cold. It was sad, but he threw it in the bin.
His mother's letter was a long one:

*Dear son I hope you are alright and healthy when you get this
letter we are OK thank God I hope you are having a good time
Robertito your cousin had a cold but that did not stop him from
being the usual heavy pest Gustavo had a fever but he's ok now
the grandparents came and made a barbecue imagine with that
fever he couldn't eat a thing Rosita wasn't too lucky with her
birthday since that morning don Pedro suddenly died like a little
bird Marta came back but was rushed to the dentist with two
abscesses she had to have penicillin and cannot eat anything with
salt for 10 days things got complicated because her blood pressure
shot up it was the day of her concert and she had already paid
for the accompanist I can imagine the good life you are having
over there with all that freedom you have I wonder if you are
looking after yourself properly you know I say you should avoid
bad influences in your life Rabbi Tapolsky asked about you I hope
you do not forget the education we have given you the students
over here have been demonstrating again what do they want I
ask myself it's not good to be so rebellious last Saturday the girls
cooked for everybody and stayed over watching tv until 2 in the
morning they made wonderful empanadas some with corn and
some with meat and also a pizza with Italian mozzarella Oh I
almost forgot Miriam and Shoshana met Damián in the street he
sends to say hello he asked them for your address and wants to
write to you if I your mother could decide your destiny I would
only ask God to bring you close to me so we can have you at our
table for the holidays if you could see me now you would not
recognise me everybody says I look great I could pass for your*

sister I swear it I wish you could change your life and work and
study more your father never studied and well there he is poor
thing when you feel anxious think of me or have dreams about
God which helps me a lot I make your bed every day and from
time to time I wash your shirts the day Argentina played against
Mexico we ate ravioli in your honour sometimes I take the bus
and look at the sky and think of you only looking at the sky can we
see each other because the sky is infinite Your mother.

At night, they continued going to Lapa, but not to the brothels.
They preferred to hang out in the bars, where they made friends
with students, writers, and artists. On some nights, they ended
up on the other side of town, at another favourite bar of theirs,
on the lake behind Ipanema. Life was generous. They didn't feel
compelled to make decisions. They dreamed of great things.
They wrote.

A couple of days before Luigi's arrival, Daniel had been
contacted by José Delmar Rocha, whom he had met once before
at the opening of an art gallery. He was a publisher of poetry
books, who also produced *Resenha* -a monthly cultural magazine;
he wanted Daniel to write a piece for him. They had arranged to
meet that afternoon. It was early for the appointment; Daniel and
Luigi had time to wander the streets.

"Why do you write?"Daniel asked Luigi.

"First, it helps me to seduce more women. Secondly, I can
discover what I feel. I don't know which is more important."

The truth was that they both knew that they wrote because
they couldn't do otherwise. They wouldn't know what else to do
with their lives.

"What about you?"

"I wanted to be a poet since my second year of high school.
We had a teacher, la Señorita Calvo, who taught us Spanish
Literature. She must have been about thirty, single and seductive,
her perfume promised a paradise beyond our reach. She had a

deep, husky voice that sent cold shivers up our spines, except for Osvaldo, who everyone called *el Bolas Tristes*-Sad Balls. "

At the back of the class, Osvaldo gave anybody, any time, a wank for free. Héctor, who years later became a Member of Parliament for the Unión Cívica Radical, was the most frequent customer. They would sit in the last row, at a double desk; Osvaldo next to the wall, Héctor on the aisle. After a while, Héctor would come into the impeccable white handkerchief he always carried in the breast pocket of his blue blazer.

"But when la Señorita Calvo came into the classroom, we all felt like masturbating."

She seemed to want to arouse them on purpose. She would read or make one of them read the most erotic poems of Pedro Salinas:

And suddenly, in the high
silence of the night,
my dreaming begins
at the border of your body …

Thirty healthy, virile, young men, dying to try the real thing, could only be thinking of the naked body of la Señorita Calvo. Jorge, who sat beside Daniel, had his own favourite poem:

Today I want to declare my love for you.
A bloody river, a sea of blood is this kiss crushed on your lips.
Your breasts are too small to summarise a story…

"She often chose Jorge to read to the class. He became completely obsessed with her, almost insane in his infatuation. He convinced himself that she fancied him."

He found out where she lived, what she did on weekends, what kind of flowers she preferred, who her favourite American actor was. Jorge tried to appear older, dressing like a businessman from the city: pinstriped suit, striped shirt, striped tie.

"His small eyes would gleam wickedly as he recited: "... *that hot flower, I'm drowning...*""

But Jorge wasn't the only one.

"I don't know how we all managed to survive those forty-five minutes, twice a week, for nine whole months. In any case, she was responsible for my writing."

"How come?"

"She was very surprised at the quality of the writing for one of my assignments. In front of the whole class, she said she thought that someone had helped me. I was speechless, outraged. I could see some of my mates grinning with pleasure, amused by my humiliation – especially Jorge. I decided to become a poet."

Rocha's office was a loft at the top of a commercial building; in the middle of a big empty space, there was an enclosure made of cheap painted wood and opaque glass, with Rocha's name as Director on the door. A few desks were arbitrarily positioned around the enclosure. On the floor, tall stacks of books stood in a miraculous balance. Daniel had always loved the smell of printed paper. It gave him a mildly intoxicated feeling. He could recognise the ink from different parts of the world, identify the country where each book had been printed. He was able to take a book, close his eyes, open it at any page and burying his face in it he would breathe deeply, "Colombia, Mexico, Argentina, Spain ...'

Rocha came out of his small office and greeted them warmly. Rocha offered them something to drink, "Coffee or *guaraná*, what would you prefer? Guaraná has magical powers! It comes from an Amazon Indian tribe, the Saterê-Maûé – wonderful people. What do you think of cities? Do you like them? I grew up in Minas Gerais, that landscape marked me forever."

Rocha and Luigi shared a Catholic upbringing: both of them had gone to Jesuit schools and both had been expelled. Rocha admired the Jesuits; according to him, they had been just about the only ones who tried to protect the Indians.

"You have to imagine the situation: either the Indians died because of the illnesses, or they were caught by the *bandeirantes.*"

"Who were the *bandeirantes?*"asked Daniel.

"Ruthless hunters who organised expeditions into the jungle to enslave them; the missions were the only refuge."

Rocha spoke of the missions as the only successful socialist project in the whole of Brazilian history; they had developed into cultural centres where work was as important as art and music. His enthusiasm was contagious.

Nobody mentioned the article that Rocha had asked Daniel to write. Instead, Luigi suggested an idea that had just occurred to him, the publication of an anthology of Argentinian poetry; he mentioned the names to be included, the poems he had in mind. Rocha liked the idea.

"Great, great! But it has to be printed in time for the Festival do Escritor Brasileiro. You could have your own stall and sell copies of the book."He wanted to know exactly how many poets they would include, how many poems, how many pages?

"Ten poets, three poems each, let's say eighty pages."

"OK! Done!"

The gods were on their side. Then, as they stood up, Rocha suggested, "We'll have a blue and white cover, the colours of your country's flag."They said warm goodbyes, as if they were old friends parting after a memorable encounter.

Luigi and Daniel leapt down the stairs. They couldn't believe their luck. They were burning with excitement, couldn't get over their amazement. "That was too much, man, just too much! I've just arrived here and we've already got an anthology to be published!'

"I'll have to send a copy to la Señorita Calvo!'

They hailed a taxi. Taxis were cheap and plentiful; the drivers were sometimes recently arrived immigrants. This one was a Syrian. It should have been easy to get to the flat; it wasn't far, and the way was not difficult. Nevertheless, the driver went all over the place, accepting no directions from "foreigners'. He insisted on being told where they were from, what they did. When he discovered they were writers, he began to recite in Arabic: there they were, stuck in terrible traffic, the meter ticking away, listening to unintelligible poems. Was this what was meant by "socialist art'?

They passed the Museu de Arte Moderna. Daniel suggested they should walk from there, but the driver wouldn't let himself be convinced that easily; he simply ignored them. "What do they need this museum for, can you tell me? They wanted to put all this art together, in one place. What is art anyway? Is art going to put food on my table? Have you ever heard of museums in the Orient? The West is all messed up, they don't know the difference between life and death, that's the problem. I'll never get used to living here; with what I earn driving this taxi, I'm able to keep my family; they live in Aleppo, all fourteen of them. I just want to make enough money to go back home rich."

Luigi asked him how long he had been in Brazil. "More than enough – twelve years,"he said. So he wasn't a recent arrival after all. He probably knew his way around the city quite well.

It was dark as they drew up to their building, Daniel asked the Syrian why he drove with his lights out. Some streets were unlit, didn't he think it was a bit dangerous?

He turned around while still driving and looked at them incredulously. "Don't you know that our Government is trying to save electricity to avoid the power cuts? I don't want to spoil their efforts, I want to contribute, it's a good government."

Putting the book of poetry together wasn't difficult. They spent the next couple of weeks writing letters, making telephone calls to Buenos Aires, correcting their manuscripts. They decided to include some of their friends in the anthology. Keen to make themselves known in another country, they were fast and efficient. They ended up with nine poets, some well known; an uneven selection, but they were pleased with the result. Rocha made sure to get it printed straight away, with the promised blue and white cover. At the same time, he had a surprise for them: he had asked Manuel Bandeira, the highly admired Modernist poet, to write a short preface.

Bandeira was enthusiastic about the anthology. He especially liked Hurtado de Mendoza's *La Burocracia de Afrodita*, which ended: ...*a mí me han arruinado las mujeres*. The evening they met him, Bandeira, who was almost eighty years old, went around repeating these lines and laughing, ""women have ruined me", how amusing! "women have ruined me...""

The Festival do Escritor Brasileiro turned out to be an extraordinary event. In the newspapers the day after, their photograph – taken at the Museu de Arte Moderna that cool Monday evening – bore little resemblance to the actual events. They showed a distorted reality, a bit like those family portraits where everybody occupies the "right place": grandparents sit in the middle, parents stand behind them, children cluster at the front. All very tidy, but not at all real.

It had started with a round table in the afternoon in which a group of intellectuals had been invited to discuss "The Engagement of the Poet in Modern Society". The meeting took place in a packed auditorium at the University. The first to speak was Imelda Portugués, professor of literature, an imposing woman of forceful convictions. A young audience followed her speech in absorbed, admiring silence. At first, Daniel too was captivated, but towards the end of her presentation it became clear that she did not think much of poets, poetry, or even literature in general. She wanted a literature that reflected reality, she said, claiming that poetry needed some social justification, it should contribute to destroying the status quo. She had obviously read her Sartre, and finished her speech shouting, "No literature! Only praxis!"It became a political rally, and the audience, mainly university students, was transported; it was a good opportunity to express their opposition to the government. Daniel was fed up; even though he sympathised with the students, he soon felt bored by the speaker's misdirected brilliance.

She was followed by Vinicius Portela, a novelist from the Northeast. A sober, composed and intelligent man, he did a good job of quietly demolishing Imelda Portugués. He argued that something essential was missing in her theories: humour. Her reasoning had been fascinating, she had dazzled them all, but literature, just as life itself, had nothing to do with logic, nor was it governed by reason. Once one took intuition, obsession and madness out of art, what was left? Darkness, death. Unfortunately, he never had a chance with the audience; after experiencing all that political fervour, they were not ready to listen. They wanted blood.

Finally, it was the poet's turn. Hildon Medeiros, an extraordinary man. He lived with his wife and two children in a small apartment in a poor area of Rio; he worked as a salesman at a furniture store to support his family. Life was hard for him, he had more than enough reasons to be drunk most of the time. When he was called to the podium, Medeiros could hardly stand up – so much *cachaça* in his veins. He approached the microphone, looked at the audience, and said, "I don't give a damn about all these words; I don't give a shit about the inane, empty, moronic farts that come out of your mouths. This is the only thing I have to say about poetry."He proceeded to undo his trousers, pulled out his dark, long, truly enormous penis, and urinated on the microphone. For a few seconds, the audience was unable to react; then, in the middle of the astounded silence, they started applauding, encouraging him to continue. Finally, a couple of guys grabbed him by the arms and took him away, wet trousers and all. After celebrating Medeiros' heroic act, the audience got up and left. No more revolutions for the time being. Meanwhile, he had been taken to the police station and charged with indecent exposure.

Although it was a spirited occasion, the evening session of the festival was quite formal: a minister, who represented the Presidente da Republica, opened the proceedings. The Argentinian ambassador and the cultural attaché were also there. Luigi and Daniel took an instant dislike to the ambassador, who was a pompous, arrogant man. Offered a book by the cultural attaché, the ambassador managed to open it at Juan Gelman's poem, entitled *Fidel*. The pretentious asshole read it out loud, glancing quickly at the cultural attaché:

> *Good night History widen your gates*
> *We're coming in with Fidel with the horse.*

Red with fury, the ambassador walked off in a huff. The cultural attaché complained, "That was stupid, if only you hadn't included the title, he would never have read the actual poem."

"If Gelman put a title on it,"Daniel argued, "who are we to take it out? He is one of the best poets of our generation. The truth is that we all admire him; in fact, we also support Fidel Castro."

Daniel couldn't follow the rest of the conversation. His attention had been caught by the crowd parting to make room for a black woman, striding towards them. She was dressed as Carmen Miranda and was making her way toward the stalls with the bearing of a queen. Everybody cheered and whistled as she passed. She had a basket of lacquered fruits on her head and smoked a cigarette through a long ivory holder. Her shiny red heels made her look very tall. She was wearing a frilled orange satin dress embroidered with sequins, and long yellow satin gloves. The red turban matched her shoes. This carnival of colours made the deep blackness of her skin even more velvety and soft. She was followed by two black women, also in brilliant shimmering dresses. The three of them belonged somewhere else, in a carnival parade, moving and dancing and weaving as if the drums of the Portela School of Samba were just behind, playing for them. There was something scandalous about the way they walked. They passed the Minister and his entourage and came straight over to the Argentinian stall. Luigi ran over to Daniel and whispered in sudden panicky excitement:

"It's the girls!"

They had completely forgotten that they had invited the transvestites; neither Daniel nor Luigi had dreamed they would come. They were delighted to see them, glad that they had found a way of participating in something they clearly felt didn't belong to them. "What are *we* going to do in a literary festival?"Socrates had said when Luigi had handed them the invitation.

The three black beauties (even the ugly Amadeu was well disguised) stood facing the stall, smiling. Stunning. Socrates grabbed the cultural attaché by the arm. "Are you the boss around here?"he enquired cheekily. "You're so handsome, so athletic, so ... how shall I put it? Robust! You know, it was those big black eyes that drew us this way."The attaché was taking it well, like a good diplomat; although obviously embarrassed by Socrates' actions, he laughed. Socrates started shouting to the public, "Come on, all of you, this is a stall selling books. Come on, buy this wonderful anthology!"And looking at the cultural attaché: "Look who we have here! Come on, this opportunity is not to be repeated."

The book sold well. Rocha was happy with their success. And the cultural attaché seemed delighted with his new friends.

Hours later, there he was, strolling along the streets of Rio with his best friend and a group of transvestites, after taking part in a writers' festival with an anthology of poetry.

Luigi and Daniel, together with Manuel, their friend in Buenos Aires, had considered themselves to be heroes of the modern era. They read Henry Miller, Jack Kerouac, and Allen Ginsberg; they wanted to be like them, *more* than them.

They studied Proudhon, admired the surrealists, and thought Rosa Luxemburg the most beautiful name in the world. They wanted to create their own narrative, something more meaningful than the empty discourse of the political parties. At that time, their lives were fragmented, scattered pieces of a jigsaw, bits and pieces that the wind could easily have blown in any direction. Inside, they felt divided, chaotic. People came and went through their lives while they felt out of place, exiled. They met every night at *El Reducto de la Flor Solar* -The Keep of the Solar Flower, a room with a bed, a couple of old desks, some bookshelves and a record player; they used it for writing, sleeping, and dreaming of better times. They tried dexedrine, listened to *Fontessa* all night, got drunk, and wrote passionate love poems. They felt they had no home but dreamed of New York, the Balearic Isles, Paris. If there was a world to be conquered, they were going to do it through drugs and poetry, sex and jazz.

What a joke.

They got to Lapa. It was a warm Monday night, and the area was rather empty. They stopped at a *churrascaria*, where the steaks were always good. By the time they had finished eating, Amadeu and Fulvio were discussing whether the Capoeira de Angola was more authentic than the Capoeira de Mestre Bimba. Amadeu was from Salvador, while Fulvio came from the tobacco plantations of Cachoeira.

"What do you know? Face it, brother, you know nothing," Fulvio argued, "Mestre Bimba created it all, *capoeira* was born in the plantations of Cachoeira, every baby born in this area comes with a *berimbau* under his arm."

"Cachoeira! Bullshit! *Capoeira* was born in Angola, and the only master is Mestre Pastinha, you hear? Your *berimbau* wasn't under you arm, you probably had it up your ass."

Fulvio and Amadeu seemed to enjoy this ritual fight where words had replaced their bodies.

The restaurant was now empty and the waiters were placing the chairs upside-down on the tables. Once they finished with dessert, Luigi suggested they leave. It had been a long day. The owner was playing a tape of traditional Portuguese *fados*, sung by Amalia Rodrigues. He shouted from behind the counter, "shame she supported that fascist bastard Salazar!"

As they left, they noticed the same pregnant adolescent prostitute that they had seen before. Sitting on the pavement, she smiled at them. Luigi approached her and gave her some money: "Why don't you go to bed? It's late."She smiled again and agreed, she would go home. Right now. She left, shouting something they could not understand.

"I doubt she has a home,"Socrates lamented.

They left Lapa and walked towards the flat. In front of a still-open bar, in the middle of the deserted street, they came across a white Mercedes limousine. The five of them stood there, spellbound by the vision of this clean, sparkling anomaly. Nobody else was around. Suddenly, Amadeu asked his friends to wait and disappeared into the bar; they could hear faint voices inside. He returned soon after, carrying something wrapped in newspaper in his hands. He climbed onto the back bumper, opened the package, and let the contents drop on to the roof of the car: it was the most enormous, thick, hard turd they had ever seen. They could never imagine anybody ever shitting it.

"This is a work of art,"said Luigi. And they all clapped.

It was difficult for them to move away from the unexpected sight, that majestic turd on top of the white limousine shining under the moonlight. Finally, they all started their way home, in silence.

3

A*migo Daniel,*
You might be surprised by this letter. I saw Miriam
and Shoshana a few days ago and they told me I could
write to you to the Consulate, so here it is. Your sisters are both
looking terrific; Miriam, so dark and intense; Shoshana, blonde
and vivacious. They are very attractive, and both are so obviously
clever!
I'm sorry I missed you before you left. The day we were supposed
to meet at La Giralda, Laura fell ill. It was a horrible flu – I
couldn't get hold of you to let you know. I had to look after her
for the following two weeks, take care of the kids, etc. She's OK
now. How are you, anyway? I've been told that the Brazilian
Government has been very generous with you, and also that
Luigi has joined you in your adventure.
Some good news: I changed jobs, and now teach History at a
secondary school in Lomas de Zamora; it's not a bad ride on the
train, in fact it's the only time I can read the newspapers. To teach
the history of our country is quite a challenge. Such an amazing
number of insignificant events! How does one teach history to
a group of adolescent boys and girls who seem permanently on

heat, only preoccupied with screwing each other, and who only
want to listen to music? Not easy. It would be tempting just to
follow the text recommended by the authorities at the Ministerio
de Educación, but I can't stand it: it's full of lies, chauvinistic
distortions, and flagrant attempts at brain-washing.
Given certain traditions in our country, I have become interested
in researching the history of repression in Latin America. I'm
finding a few surprises: while the religious, judicial and secular
powers in Spain were quite happy to justify all forms of abuse,
Bartolomé de las Casas was about the only one who opposed them,
openly denouncing the excesses committed by the Spaniards all
over America. But the task is massive. I'll have to be careful, for
example, in trying to be scrupulous in gathering the information.
I'll have to be frugal too – there is so much about the Inquisition!
And I don't want to get lost in that period. This has taken me
a few centuries back, beyond the time of the Spanish Conquest.
What is quite clear already is this: not much has changed since
the Romans, when torture was part of the procedures followed by
the judges. Nice, don't you think?
In Argentina, there was always torture. Reading this material
makes me shiver; in the 30s, La Legión Cívica tortured and
murdered people, supported by Uriburu and his government.
Uriburu's fascism continued during the presidency of Justo, who
refused asylum to many scientists trying to escape from Hitler.
Do you remember when we were kids, during Perón's time?
Everybody spoke of la picana and of the political activists who
were tortured in jail. My old man, like your own father, was a
member of the U.C.R. I lived in fear that he'd be taken away. I
have been reading the accounts of the parliamentary discussions
of 1953. I discovered that Santiago Nudelman, a congressman,
denounced the acts of torture with plenty of details. And now,
after eighteen months in power, our new self-proclaimed Head of
State, The Big Moustache Onganía wants to dictate the way we
dress, how I should cut my hair, and whether girls are allowed to

wear bikinis. He has become a dictator, persecuting and torturing his political adversaries.

Well, I am in a crisis. Teaching, which I hate, helps me to survive. Finding the time to write novels is hard and hardly pays the rent. A book about repression might not even reach the printers. Why am I not rich and famous? I know you're dreadful at writing letters so I won't necessarily expect an answer. Do something else! Send a postcard instead – of the girls of Ipanema, NOT of Pelé, please. A big hug.

Chau,
Damián

4

They lived a double life. During the day, the world of culture: the poets, the painters, the local dilettanti. Late at night, they sought refuge in other places: the bohemians, the wasted, the famished. What did they want? They didn't even ask themselves. But it was in Lapa that they felt most alive. That night, like so many others, they walked around the streets aimlessly, talking, making jokes, stopping at different bars for a beer.

"Tonight, I feel like dancing, let's go dance samba and pick up some girls."

"What a wonderful idea, *Danny,*"Luigi teased him. The only person that called him that was Lola.

They stopped at the entrance to a colonial house that had been converted into a dance hall. The doors were wide open. Luigi and Daniel climbed the stairs by threes and fours, racing each other. On the dance floor, a drunk was falling over while dancing by himself. A whore appeared from behind the bar, her nearly bare breasts jiggling. She lurched towards the drunk, singing:

Arturo, Arturo,
we love you, silly boy...

She improvised the lyrics, singing the tune coming from the speakers. He managed to embrace her, resting his head on her breasts; dancing together, they moved across the floor. As they approached, Luigi and Daniel could see the colourful tattoos covering the woman's breasts: butterflies, flowers, little birds. Arms around each other, the whore holding up the lurching drunk, the strange couple was like a Madonna with Child, *carioca* style.

There was nothing in the dance-hall for them, only a few made-up old ladies sitting around a table at the end of the room. They were getting ready to leave when a young black woman appeared. She wore a loose flowery shirt and carried her cigarettes in one of its front pockets; her white trousers were so tight that they clearly showed the lace edging of her tiny knickers. Her presence lit up the hall. Leaning on the railing that separated the stairs from the dance floor, she appeared to be looking for somebody. Daniel could smell her perfume and felt an urge to kiss her neck. He was ready to fall in love at once with an unknown prostitute from Lapa.

By way of starting a conversation, Luigi asked her the price of entry, how much were the drinks. He had also been touched: in trying to speak Portuguese, everything he said came out in Italian. She responded with a smile, looking first at Luigi and then at Daniel. Two big, black, perfectly round eyes, shone in contrast to her dark skin. "Just for one of you, or for the two?" They burst into laughter, which disconcerted her. Instead of trying to clarify the misunderstanding, Daniel took one of her hands and she pressed his firmly. Luigi did the same with the other. She didn't know what they wanted from her. "My name is Wanda," announced the black goddess. The three of them walked down the stairs still holding hands, with Wanda skipping between the two men.

A real happening in the middle of the midnight jungle.

It was Friday night, a soccer match had just finished at the Maracaná stadium. Groups of high-spirited teenagers were roaming up and down the streets, hoping for some action. Girls. Or fights. With luck, perhaps both.

Wanda wanted to know, "Who are you? What are your names? What do you do?'

"Ah,"Luigi said, "*that*'s a secret, you can't tell it to anybody. We're smugglers and bring American cigarettes, French perfumes, Swiss watches and British tea into the country."

Wanda was enchanted; she liked their cockiness, although it wasn't certain that she believed them.

"We also import exotic Turkish condoms with strange shapes at the tip,"Daniel added, "German biscuits in decorated tins, Italian nylon stockings. We have a deal with the captain of a Greek cargo boat; all the merchandise is brought to the port of Santos."

"Could I have a pair of stockings for free?'

"Of course! A dozen of them!"

"We should try to get another girl, I have a friend who will like you."They agreed, somewhat reluctantly.

They walked for a while until they reached a small square. It was late but the heat kept people awake, either on the street or on their balconies. They sat out on the pavement on wooden chairs with woven straw seats, watching TV through open French doors, the sets in each living room at full volume. It was a deafening swirl of voices, loud music, laughter and children's cries.

Wanda approached one of the houses and shouted her friend's name. "Fernandinha! Fernandinha!"It was a miracle she could be heard. A tall, rather too thin white woman appeared at the window. She had big plastic curlers in her hair covered with a headscarf, and continued varnishing her nails while seemingly arguing with Wanda. Luigi and Daniel couldn't understand a word of what the women said. Finally, Wanda came back to where they had been waiting. "She's given all these conditions; she has only an hour to spare; I think she's in a bad mood, another time."

"We only want you, Wanda,"exclaimed Luigi.

She gave them a glorious smile, placed both of her arms around their necks, and whispered: "It'll be great, just the three of us."

Wanda insisted on going to the Praça Mauá, so they hailed a taxi. She talked all the way, teased them, made silly jokes, told them stories about her fellow workers, and argued fervently with the driver about which soccer team was the best. She supported Flamengo, the taxi-driver Fluminense.

"But you're wasting your time with these lousy Brazilian teams,"Daniel exclaimed. "You have to admit it, the best team in the world is Boca Juniors."

It was funny to see Wanda so involved in a discussion about soccer, but all of a sudden she shut up and then confessed, "I have a headache, it's killing me."They stopped at an all-night *drogaria* and got some aspirin; the driver offered her cool orange juice from a flask, and she soon came to life again.

"One day we should go to a soccer match together,"she said, "it's like a mini Carnival. The Maracaná holds two hundred thousand people!'

"Never!"Luigi made the mistake of saying. "Come on, it's only a hundred thousand."

"That's the official figure!"the taxi driver retorted, offended. "The truth is double that, everybody knows it."

"Of course it's two hundred! People go completely crazy before, during, and after the match; they drink *cachaça*, play drums, light firecrackers, and they even sacrifice chickens; they cut their throats for good luck and then throw them on to the pitch."

"We'll definitely go,"said Daniel.

They got off at a corner by an old colonial church. Hundreds of white candles of all sizes were burning on the pavement, on the steps to the main entrance, on the windowsills. Beggars slept curled up in corners, seemingly everywhere; they looked like corpses in the yellow light. Wanda stood in front of the church for a few minutes, seemingly studying each of the beggars' faces. "I hate poverty,"she murmured. Then she jumped in front of Daniel, held him tightly and started dancing, forcing him to follow her, away from the beggars, the church, the candles.

At the next corner, she stopped and waited for Luigi. As he approached, she stood in front of him, legs apart, arms akimbo. She threw a few punches at his stomach, imitating a rough boxer. He embraced her and kissed her on the cheek. "What are we doing here, anyway?"Daniel could hear jealousy in his voice and hoped it wasn't too obvious.

"We are going to get some *maconha*,"she whispered. They all laughed, maybe once again for different reasons. Luigi and Daniel didn't believe her, they thought it was a joke; back in their own country, marihuana was not yet that well known, nor was it that widely used.

After a few blocks, they got to a deserted street – except for a figure at the other end, barely visible, leaning against a wall, his cigarette smoke betraying his presence. Wanda told Luigi to wait. She walked slowly towards the guy, followed by Daniel. Wanda signalled to Daniel to stop and crossed the street alone; she took some money out of her purse and placed it behind a water pipe coming down from a balcony in a house at the other side of the road. After rejoining Daniel, they retraced their steps. Next, they all sat down on the pavement, still warm from a day of relentless sun. The dealer finished his cigarette and walked over to the pipe, pulled out the bundle of notes, counted them and put them in his pocket. He took off his straw hat, pulled something out and left it where the money had been. Then, the man disappeared round the next corner, walking away languidly, his hat cocked on his head. The stuff of B movies.

Wanda got up and jumped in the air, shouting with happiness. It was as if Flamengo had scored a goal; her cries could be heard far away, reverberating through the silent streets. Daniel was sure she woke everybody up in the neighbourhood and for the first time he thought of the police. Wanda ran to the spot where the dope had been left, put it in her bra and came back to them, whistling. A little girl with a new toy.

"Don't take it so seriously," she said to Daniel, lightly elbowing him in the stomach. "We're together, remember?" He didn't know what she had seen in his face. "I'm not afraid," he said. It was about two o'clock in the morning when they finally made it to the flat. They couldn't stop giggling. They didn't want to wake Socrates and his friends but it was difficult to keep quiet. Once inside the room she took great care to investigate every corner, open every drawer, look under the bed, peep out the window, examine their books of poetry. In one of the drawers she found a few condoms. She took one out, undid the packet and blew it up; she made a knot at the end and started batting it about like a balloon. They all got into the game, jumping on the bed, standing on the sofa. Every time Wanda hit the balloon, she screamed and howled and laughed at the top of her voice. She made all sorts of animal noises: cackles and squeals, twitters and whistles. Luigi and Daniel joined this crazy concert.

Not surprisingly, Socrates appeared at the door of their room, wrapped in his red silk *robe de chambre*, angry and ready to snap someone's head off. He stood there, not a word, staring at Wanda. Beside himself with rage, he looked magnificent in his fury. Wanda broke the silence, blurting out: "It's my fault, woman, I'm sorry, I'm really, really sorry." Luigi and Daniel kept quiet. But Socrates was not going to be easily appeased; he simply turned on his heels and slammed the door behind him.

Wanda sat in the middle of the bed and started rolling a joint. "Don't pay any attention. Jealousy, pure jealousy. Have you ever tried this?" she asked them, lowering her voice, her black eyes sparkling with mischief. They hadn't. They had never seen a joint being made before: she stuck two cigarette papers together with spit, added another at the top, sprinkled the dried marihuana leaves inside, and rolled it all with great skill. She lit up and inhaled, holding the smoke in her lungs. She showed them how to block their noses and their mouths with their hands, to help them hold the smoke as long as they could. She offered it to Luigi; he imitated her and then passed it to Daniel, who did the same. They were sitting in a circle on the bed and the joint went around a few more times. Daniel got up, lit a candle and turned off the main light.

Wanda told them that she had been born on the outskirts of Manaus, in the Amazon, on the northern bank of the Rio Negro. Anselmo, her father, had always been against holding a job and eked out a living selling medicinal herbs; her mother worked as a maid and earned just enough to keep the family ticking over from one week to the next. Wanda's family belonged to the strangest of cults; the devotees had as their main saint a Rabbi Moyal, who had come originally from Jerusalem, hired by the small Jewish community of Manaus. He had died at the beginning of the twentieth century – most likely, the only rabbi to have lived in that city.

Over many years, the rabbi's grave in the general cemetery had become a popular shrine. People placed rosary beads on his tombstone – instead of the traditional Jewish pebbles – to ask for miracles. Wanda's father claimed that the healing powers of his plants came from the beads "blessed"by the dead rabbi.

After every expedition into the jungle to collect the herbs, her father came back in a terrible mood, complaining about the mosquitoes and the snakes. Cursing his fate, he tied the plants in bunches and hung them upside down in the patio to dry. Then, he ate two whole barbecued chickens under the Tree of Heaven (which his own grandfather had planted in the back garden), helped by a whole bottle of *cachaça*. Finally, he slept non-stop for two days in the hammock on the veranda. When he awoke, Anselmo would bathe in the old tin tub in warm water scented with wild flowers, and then put on his best white Egyptian cotton shirt that a friend had brought him from Leticia, up-river in Colombia. Afterwards, he sat on the front porch of their house displaying his medicines on a tattered and moth-eaten card table. Wanda was the one he chose to help him with sales.

Wanda's father had a soft voice, big, dark, intense eyes, and always smoked a white clay pipe filled to the brim with his own mixture of herbal tobacco. He had learnt everything he knew about plants from his grandmother, who still lived with the family. Many people would consult him for different complaints and illnesses; Anselmo always felt reluctant to charge any money for it.

On one of his trips through the villages along the river, he bought a one-eyed fighting cock, El Pirata. Rosa, Wanda's mother, in a moment of inexplicable ontological confusion, mistook the cock for a chicken and was just about to cook him for the evening meal. Anselmo managed to stop her right before she twisted the poor animal's neck a final time, but it remained bent for ever. Rosa, filled with remorse, never forgave herself for this terrible blunder. El Pirata became her favourite, the creature could do no wrong.

Whenever she was asked to sell plants with her father, Wanda felt a mixture of great pleasure and dread; she was fascinated by the sight of the big, powerful, corpulent man sitting in a small cane chair at the front of the house. Although never profitable, the plants had provided her father with a certain reputation. Wanda felt totally drawn into a world of riddles and mystery. She loved seeing how he took each specimen and with great tenderness separated the entangled roots, studying them with a broken magnifying glass attached to a torch. Later, when Wanda started going to school, she learned a few names from a book on Brazilian flora: *parvifolia, muricata, suaveolens, argenteomarginata* … Those botanical names repeated on rainy afternoons to learn her lessons made her feel protected and loved.

Wanda's story didn't have a happy ending: she became pregnant at fifteen and her father threw her out of the house. Following their adopted Jewish customs, he declared her dead.

He covered all the mirrors in the house, lit candles and placed a glass of water and a white cloth at his bedroom window.

Wanda was saved by one of the middle-class women who employed her mother. She took her to a doctor (one of the lady's secret lovers) who performed an abortion for free. Then the woman gave Wanda the address of her own daughter in Rio, and put her on a coach to the big city. The rest was predictable: Wanda was soon picked up and seduced by a pimp, who forced her to work for him.

As he listened to the story, a warm, peaceful sensation pervaded Daniel's body; he felt very close to Wanda and yet something in his mind was pulling him away. Soon he became two bodies and two minds, the good feelings towards her were accompanied by an intense impulse to run away; he wanted to dissolve and disappear into Wanda, burning with desire, but he was also paralysed with fear, intimidated. The memory of Lola came back to haunt him –a ghost returning to reclaim him. He forced himself to look Lola in the face, confront her once and for all, but it was Wanda who was holding his face between her hands, kissing him tenderly.

Suddenly he got up and went to the bathroom. He looked at himself in the mirror. His skin was full of spiders, and the itching was unbearable. He stuck his tongue out: miniature *germánicas* were crawling all over; his hair was moving like a big, black animal. He ordered himself not to panic: "What's the worst that can happen to you? That you'll shit in your pants?"He laughed. The thought inspired him. Sitting on the toilet, he thought he understood the perfect circle of Nature, the Order of the Universe. Maybe there was something special in this sacred herb, real wisdom could perhaps be attained through it. He felt better when he was finished. From the bathroom to the bedroom next door there wasn't much distance; nevertheless, as far as he was concerned, it became comparable to scaling the Obelisco.

In the room, Luigi was reading from the bilingual edition of Quasimodo's poems. Daniel had never heard him reciting in Italian before:

The pink moon, the wind,
your colour of woman of the North,
the expanse of snow...

"He told me the truth: you're not smugglers, you're poets!"exclaimed Wanda. "You are going to be famous poets, like Vinicius."

"No, Wanda, *he* is the poet,"said Luigi. His voice sounded sarcastic.

"And *he* is the real writer,"Daniel added, with a pinch of resentment.

Wanda asked them to take all their clothes off. She did the same and turned off the light. Lying sideways, she clamped her legs around his waist and murmured: "Take me."She didn't need to beg him.

It was only afterwards that Daniel remembered Luigi, at the other side of Wanda. Daniel decided to leave them and lay down on the floor, improvising a bed with a couple of sleeping bags. He lit a cigarette.

He must have fallen asleep, he couldn't remember when Wanda had come down to lie beside him. She was looking at him. "My *cafetão* is hopeless, he's a loser, he's ruined, a delinquent. Imagine, what kind of future can I expect with a pimp who is a car thief? What life is there for me, protected by a crook? I need another man, I want to start a family."

She had tears in her eyes and yet she was also smiling, obviously happy: "My love, my lover, do you want to be my *cafetão*?'

Wanda. Little Brown Sugar.

Daniel woke up to Luigi's snoring. Wanda was on his right, still asleep, her naked back against his arm. Daniel remembered a dream: he was in his grandmother's house, a small apartment at the back of their shop. In the dream, he was young, perhaps eleven or twelve, and his head had been shaved. His grandmother was cooking something in a frying pan.

The morning light slowly filled the room. He lay on the improvised bed on the floor, thinking. Why had his grandmother appeared in his dream?

Daniel fumbled for the packet of cigarettes. He whimpered: his right shoulder ached and he must have slept badly. Sleeping on the floor wasn't that great after all. Wanda woke up; she turned around to look at him. She stretched and smiled. "Hi!"he said, stroking her face. She got hold of his hand and kissed it. The smell of cooking came through the window: so that explained the frying pan of the dream! Wanda, still holding his hand, asked him whether he believed in reading palms.

"Didn't you know that all poets are a bit prophetic?"said Daniel. "We cast lots, consult the I-Ching, decode the secret messages shaped by gathering clouds, what do you want to know? Just ask me."

"What's the I-Ching?'

"A very old Chinese system of fortune-telling."

"Please, read my palm,"Wanda urged him.

"Did you know who invented the art of reading palms?"Daniel asked her. Wanda shook her head. "Also the Chinese! It isn't just the lines, everything else should also be taken into account for a proper interpretation of the future: for example, the shape of your hand, or the length of your fingers."

Daniel sat up, held her right hand and closely examined the lines on her palm.

"Can you see how curved these lines are? Your wrist is narrow, but your palm bulges out. You have long and delicate fingers; your fingertips are rounded and gentle. This hand denotes someone sensitive and intelligent. Your line of fate reaches the Mount of Saturn, which is a very good sign."He predicted a happy marriage, three children, a long life. With inspiration, anyone can spin a story.

Just then, Luigi woke up. "What's that smell?"he asked. "And so early in the morning!"

"It's chicken,"guessed Daniel.

"It is,"said Wanda.

"They fry it first in oil and then make a sauce with blood – the blood, of course, being the most important ingredient."He went on being inspired by the previous reading of Wanda's hands. "It's a secret recipe, only poets can gain access to it, Vinicius told me about it."

"What a lot of bullshit!"Luigi laughed.

Daniel could have said that God was a rare bird from the Amazon and that the world had been created through its arse, Wanda would have been tempted to believe him.

When they finally came out of their room, a Council of War was waiting for them. Socrates, Amadeu and Fulvio were all dressed straight as men –something unthinkable a few hours earlier. This was serious business, no more beauty queen stuff. Was it so unforgivable to have brought a woman into the flat? Perhaps Wanda's presence in itself was more of an insult than the incredible racket they had made the previous night. One thing was clear: they had been judged and condemned. Socrates suggested that they leave the flat. "The sooner the better; don't mess with me!"He sounded threatening; no more friendliness. Daniel was reminded of the first time Socrates opened the door of the flat, how aggressive he had seemed then. They didn't have a clue how those guys earned their living. Maybe they weren't only transvestites involved in some Black Church, maybe they were criminals.

Without a word they went back into their room and started stuffing things into suitcases. Too many things. Their library had grown larger; a lot of the writers they had met in those weeks had given them copies of their books. Wanda, who had followed them, was subdued and felt responsible for what was happening.

"Forget it,"Daniel said to her, "they can go and fuck themselves."

"A bunch of queers,"Luigi couldn't stop complaining. Daniel hoped they couldn't hear him.

"What are you going to do?"asked Wanda.

"Move,"Daniel said, impatiently.

"I hated this place anyway,"Luigi muttered. Nobody believed him.

The Brazilians were shut in their own rooms when they left. No farewell party then. Luigi stood in the middle of the living room and recited in a loud voice, as if giving a sermon: "...for love is strong as death; jealousy, cruel as the grave."Remnants from the seminary.

Once in the street, they bought the *Jornal do Brasil* and sat on a bench in the Parque do Flamengo to study the classified ads. They were under a jacaranda, its feathery shadow protecting them from the sun. Daniel had always felt a certain passion for that tree; he liked the masses of bell-shaped flowers that came out in the spring, a big mauve cloud; he enjoyed looking at the irregular outline of the trunk and branches against the sky, the lavender carpet of fallen flowers after the rains. Above all, he liked the name: *ja-ca-ran-dá*, a Portuguese word which he enjoyed pronouncing in Spanish, while at the same time playing with the vowels: *jequerendé; jiquirindí; jocorondó; jucurundú*.

In the newspaper there were plenty of rooms and flats available; it was a matter of deciding which part of the city they wanted to live in. Daniel preferred to remain close to Lapa; Luigi felt like a change, he wanted to move nearer the beaches.

"That's for tourists,"Daniel argued, "for tourists and rich people, I've been there, I'm not going back, it'll be fun closer to town."

Wanda moved away from the bench, unconcerned about the argument. Skinny, starving cats quickly surrounded her. She picked up a couple, talking to them and stroking them. Daniel saw nothing wonderful about playing with feral, flea-ridden cats. "Leave the bloody cats alone,"he yelled. Wanda looked at him with sad eyes, dropped the cats on the ground, and walked away. So much for his new romantic liaison. He was behaving as if they were a long-suffering married couple. "Are you going to let her go, just like that? You can't be such an idiot, *boludo!*"Luigi shouted, as he started after Wanda. Daniel stayed put, obstinately glued to the bench, watching them both disappear in the distance.

Daniel waited for them. After an hour, they hadn't come back. Now, what? A phrase came to his mind: *Your passion rolls the dice with the body of your certainty.* He wrote it down in his notebook.

Daniel felt irritated about what had happened with the transvestites, but he didn't care all that much. Instead, he was thinking about Damián's letter; his friend's comments about the political situation in Argentina troubled him. Was Onganía turning into a dictator? Damián was writing about the history of repression in Latin America –that couldn't make the authorities too happy. Yes, that letter had made him feel worried, depressed, *mufado.*

He looked around: people had invaded the park with their footballs and transistor radios. He felt self-conscious with the two suitcases at his feet, the loose sheets of newspaper flying about, dozens of hungry cats around him, wailing, rubbing up against his legs, annoying him with their demands for food. He got up, folded the pages of classified ads, picked up the heavy baggage and started walking towards the restaurant on the hill. He would study the advertisements again, decide on a flat he liked, make the necessary telephone calls from the restaurant. Fuck Wanda. The hell with Luigi.

Daniel was mostly concerned not to look too much like a lost tourist. He had already heard enough tales of violence against foreigners in the streets; he didn't want to take any risks. He was feeling needlessly conscious of having smoked *maconha* the previous night; it was illegal and its use was harshly penalised. For him, it had been a sensational experience, he had never known anything like it. While stoned, he had kept a precarious and delicate balance, as if walking a tightrope, and yet there had been something sublime in it all. Now that he could recognise the smell, he also realised that everybody smoked it everywhere: in theatres, at open-air concerts, in cinemas, at the beach. In contrast to this apparent social tolerance, the police were very heavy-handed with anyone they caught. Daniel couldn't swear that he wasn't walking around that morning with *maconha* written in luminous paint on his forehead. The last place he wanted to spend a holiday was in a Rio jail.

From where he sat in the restaurant, the beach stretched down below like a wonderful ribbon of sand around the Bay of Guanabara. Daniel couldn't understand how the *cariocas* managed to make it to the beach at all hours of the day, every day. They played football, swam, and lay in the sun, weekdays or holidays. Luigi and Daniel had been warned about the pollution in those waters: all the beaches around the centre were the recipients of the city's sewage and some industrial waste. But the *cariocas* simply ignored what they were supposed to know, and played in the water as much as on the sand.

Studying the ads, a couple of them drew his attention: a student commune wanted new members, an artist had a room to spare. He had never heard of a commune; it intrigued him. But the attraction of the ads was the location: they were both in the morro de Santa Teresa. Daniel had been up there in the open tram that went over the old aqueduct from the centre. In the hills, old colonial houses built on cobblestoned streets had once been the homes of the upper classes. Around these grand mansions, the poor started building their *favelas*, often with the best views. The higher up, the more dangerous those shanty towns became. This was where the outlaws of Rio lived: the Mafiosi, pimps, thugs, burglars, escaped convicts and pickpockets – they came in all shapes and sizes. With time, the rich had moved away, and a new population of students, artists, musicians and writers had come to fill their houses. The idea of going up and down everyday on the *bondinho* with this mixed bag of people had great appeal.

He should have guessed: the public telephone at the restaurant was out of order. Having carried the suitcases full of books all the way up the hill, he was thrown by this minor setback. He sat back, thinking, "Where was it that words were called *portmanteaux*? Maybe in Lewis Carroll?"He kept on looking at the suitcases trying to imagine them full of meanings, implications, connotations, misunderstandings and contradictions. His love of poetry was based on a fascination with words, not only for what they might be able to communicate in a clear, precise way, but also for what they could suggest and evoke through their ambiguities. Words could tell the truth, and yet mislead and conceal.

He wrote in his notebook: *The very impossibility of a metaphor confronts you with the strange passion present in the desire to write.* He imagined writing as a mock physical fight with the *portmanteaux*-words, it was a ridiculous image: Johnny Weismüller having it out with rubber crocodiles in the fake African lagoons of the early Tarzan movies. As much as he loved words, he also wanted to destroy them, spoil them, force them to reveal their falsehood. But the *portmanteaux*-words always won the battle. He recited:

> *The earth is blue like an orange*
> *Never a mistake words don't lie…*

Those lines of Paul Eluard were just about the only thing he could remember in French.

Daniel walked away from the restaurant dragging the suitcases. He began to feel defeated, a child lost in the jungle.

Pathetic. He finally found a public phone in working order. Outside the booth, he sat on one of the suitcases waiting for two mulatto girls to finish their call. They had all the time in the world, why hurry? They gossiped on, giggling and exclaiming; from time to time, they looked at him, rolling their eyes and making faces; they shrieked with laughter, jeering at him. He sat there, indifferent, impervious to all the fuss. What started as drizzle became torrential rain. He didn't move. Maybe the girls in the booth would now feel even less motivated to hang up. He composed a short phrase in his mind: *Rain – Like death: without it, nothing new will be created.* He took out a pen and wrote it in his notebook, protecting it with his hands so it wouldn't get wet. He added a note at the end: *to be developed.*

Such grandiosity.

The rain stopped as quickly as it had begun. It occurred to him that the girls might have fiddled the phone; he hadn't seen them put any money in for a long while. Perhaps they hadn't even been talking to anybody at all, maybe they had been faking the whole thing. He suddenly became inflamed with resentment and frustration, and started banging on one side of the booth. They hung up at once, left the booth, and ran off jubilantly.

"A real party at your expense, you sucker!"he said to himself.

The number of the commune was engaged, so he tried the artist. A woman answered. She was a painter and lived with her four-year-old son in a big house, where she had her own studio; she had one room to spare, she explained, with a view over the mountains. Daniel told her a bit about himself and didn't mention Luigi at all. The painter gave him the address. As he wrote it down and listened to the instructions of how to find her house, he saw a dilapidated van pull up right by the phone booth. A lad jumped out, picked up the suitcases and threw them into the back; he leapt back in and the van took off, immediately swallowed up by the traffic. The whole thing took two seconds.

Daniel was stunned. He dropped the handset and stepped out of the booth; he walked around it twice, looking for the suitcases. He couldn't believe they weren't there any more. Back inside the booth, he heard the woman shouting at the other end of the line: "*Oi! Oi!* Hallo! Hallo! Speak, *meu Deus*, speak, for Christ's sake."He couldn't say a word. She obviously realised that something was wrong and didn't hang up. After a pause, he picked up the handset and managed to whisper: "Yes, yes, it's OK – *ta ótimo*. It's just that somebody has stolen my suitcases, that's all, nothing serious, really."

"Oh, is that all?"

"Yes, that's all."

They both fell silent again. Then Daniel said: "I've got your directions, I'll be there as soon as I can."

The shock of the theft didn't last long. He felt a certain admiration for those kids; they made it look so easy. He checked the contents of his shoulder bag: ID card, money, address book, cigarettes, notebook – everything essential was there. He tried to remember the contents of his suitcase but couldn't, except for the books; he knew he would miss them. For the first time, he would be travelling light in the world. He shouldn't regret it, there would be few opportunities in life to start anew, without any possessions.

5

Querido Daniel,

The postcard of the girl on the beach was great! And your letter was very encouraging. You surprised me: you do write letters after all! Thanks. I need all the support I can get. The photograph of Luigi and you at the Festival – I must say – is very impressive, I'm looking forward to reading the anthology.

It's midnight now, I'm writing this letter while Laura and the kids are asleep. I've just come back from a rowdy meeting at the Teachers' Union: when people are hungry they get desperate; they might go crazy or get violent. You must be worried about the situation in Brazil. Last week I read an article in Marcha by a guy called Souza Barros, do you know him? The statistics he quoted are appalling: 4% of the population controls 50% of the wealth; 4,000,000 are malnourished; thousands of abandoned children in the streets; for each dollar earned exporting bananas, only 11 cents remain in the country. And yet, the political situation can't be as bad as it is here, in our beloved country.

Death has become an obsession; we have an invasion of posters in the streets: Evita Perón, Juan Manuel de Rosas, Felipe Vallese, el Ché Guevara. Is this a prophetic vision of the future? Are we falling in love with death? Are we predestined to end up in a civil war? I'm not sure. I go on enjoying my reading and my writing – more than anything else in this world. It's an individual and solitary activity, a selfish pleasure of which my "committed" friends seriously disapprove. But as you can see, I still go to Union meetings, I try to participate: if we have to descend into Hell, I'd rather be heard. It occurred to me that Argentina is a phantasmagoria, a Joycean mirage that only plagiarism could reflect. I can't justify this statement just now.

My students continue to give me a certain amount of satisfaction, but I fear for them: they've started on the university students but even secondary school kids are not safe from persecution. The manuscript for the book on the history of repression is limping along; how can I deal with the past, when I can hardly cope with the present? Our new dictator Onganía turned out to be an authoritarian caudillo, ascetic, as strict as he is constipated. He has formed a completely Catholic government, and a lot of them are nationalists. Do you know who Mario Amadeo is, a supporter of the Guardia Restauradora Nacionalista? A great friend of Big Moustache. If I were Jewish, this would worry me. Another anti-Semite is in charge of the police. Furthermore, the Director of Secret Services is Eduardo Señorans, who has protected members of Tacuara from arrest for anti-Semitic violence. There have been a number of official raids in the Once and in calle Libertad. Is there another Tragic Week of 1919 in the making? Too many Jews were killed then, what's going to happen now?

Do you remember Sergio Kustin? He now lives in the States. He sent me a clipping from The New York Times; they compare this Government's tactics with Hitler's troops in the 30s. I have a cousin who emigrated to Australia; he's a qualified doctor but isn't allowed to practise; he opened a bakery in Sydney and now sells South American pastries: medialunas, cuernitos y bolas de fraile. He's asked me to join him. We seem to be condemned forever to be governed and controlled by ruffians and thugs (although our President cannot be described exactly as such).

Of course, my cousin's invitation is tempting! But how can I leave my friends and relatives? I can't stand the idea of my two children growing up in a foreign country, speaking a different language. Buenos Aires is the city I love, where I've learned el duro oficio de vivir. Anyway, enough of this. I hope that the "dangerous" books we hid for you have reached you by now; your mother came to collect them a while ago. Keep in touch. Regards to Luigi. I know Laura wanted to send you a kiss. A big hug.

Chau,

Damián

6

The weather was hot and humid, stifling. As the *bondinho* moved slowly up the mountain, the rain started again. For many years, every time it rained – not just a shower or a dull winter drizzle, but the real tropical, violent, torrential rains of hot summer afternoons – Daniel inevitably remembered the lines from Raúl González Tuñón's poem:

We knew then that the rain was also beautiful.
Sometimes, it falls gently and one thinks of abandoned cemeteries.
At other times, it falls with fury, and one thinks of tidal waves that
have devoured so many wonderful islands with strange names...

The tram was almost empty. A few women, on their way back from the market with heavy bags of shopping, sat on the narrow benches in silence. In that heat, talking was a big effort. Daniel managed to get off at the right stop and found the house without difficulty. As soon as the woman opened the door, she started shouting at him:

"I'm Olinda Morais. It's time you arrived, I'm completely fed up with this situation, I've complained many times to no avail, they think I'm crazy, I wasted a whole day at the Water Resources Commission, and another whole afternoon talking to this moron at the Sanitation Department who sent me to see a colleague of his, another jerk at the Water Supply office of the Council who was like the rest – fucking useless. What else am I supposed to do? You tell me, I want to know, do you have any real authority to deal with this or not? If women ran the world, things would be much better, I assure you. Come, follow me, see for yourself."

She hadn't allowed him to say one word. Olinda was short, had olive skin and big eyes. She moved with quick, precise gestures, an ambiguous but attractive mixture of nerves and sensuality. In spite of her anger, her green eyes communicated generosity and tenderness. Her black hair hung in an untidy plait, ready to unravel. She took Daniel by the hand, firmly, as if he were a child; he let himself be guided like a blind man through the incredible mess of papers, books and records in her living room.

Olinda took him to the bathroom. Stunned by her verbal deluge, Daniel perversely began to enjoy this obvious misunderstanding. She hadn't stopped talking all the way through the long dark corridor.

"I've never seen anything like it,"she complained, "nothing, nothing like this."

She pointed out the green fungus that grew in every corner and climbed the bathtub and the walls. The stench of damp was unbearable; it had been made worse by the sweet incense that Olinda lit to disguise it. She wouldn't stop talking. "The water comes up through every plughole; instead of draining, the water comes out of these holes! How do you explain this, tell me? I'm fed up: first, I don't have any proper running water, and then, I have to dry this place every day."

She started telling him something about her grandmother, how she had a similar problem in her village. But Daniel had stopped listening. It wasn't his day, he should have tried the commune. And yet, he thought, this woman isn't crazy; she had seemed nice and generous on the phone.

And those green eyes.

When he started paying attention again, Olinda was saying, "… the water kept running up the plughole in the kitchen and up all the waste pipes in her house."

"Whose house?"

"My grandmother's!"

"Ah, right."

"The water is supposed to go down the holes, not come up them; how do you explain this? My grandma finally called a priest to exorcise the house. And it worked!"

"I'm pleased to hear it,"Daniel finally said with exaggerated courtesy. But his only thought was: "How am I going to get out of this?"

"So, do you have anything to say about this?"Olinda suddenly asked him. She glared into his eyes, demanding an answer. What was he supposed to do? Maybe he could help her to get an exorcist.

"Look, I'm sure we can fix it,"Daniel heard himself saying.

"Good, I trusted you as soon as I opened the door."

A few seconds later he was outside her house, feeling crushed. Olinda closed the door behind him with a smile. Daniel may have been knocked out but this was only the first round. He came back with a loud bang on the door. Olinda opened it wide and Daniel charged in, this time striking the first blow. It wasn't just Olinda: he was throwing punches at the transvestites, the girls at the public telephone, the guys who had stolen the suitcases, and Onganía – the Big Moustache, the Walrus.

"Don't you open your mouth until I say you can. Have you ever lost your suitcases? Well, I don't care whether you have or not but I've just lost everything I own, can you bloody hear me?'

It took a fraction of a second. Olinda burst into loud infectious laughter and suddenly they were both in stitches. When she recovered, Olinda disappeared into the kitchen and came back with a bowl of chopped fruit: peaches, plums, watermelon, and his favourite, *abacaxí*. It wasn't just the fruit, it was also the word: *abacaxí*. It sounded like the name of some generous and protective god of *candomblé*. The word conjured up in Daniel's mind all those other names the Indians had given to the jungle plants, their delectable fruits and astonishing animals. It was possible that the word itself had created the incredible taste of the pineapple. Eating *abacaxí* in Rio brought him close to Paradise.

Olinda Morais' paintings hung on every wall of the house. A lot of them were of the *sertão*, the forsaken deserts of the Northeast, where she came from. It turned out that Olinda was a much admired painter in her country, both in her capacity as an artist and for her commitment to the Communist Party; this had led to her spending a few lonely nights in jail. She knew the history of the *Nordeste* well. While sitting on the floor of the sitting-room, she told him about the *cangaceiros*, the bandits from the *sertão*, legendary romantic figures who were supposed to steal from the rich and give to the poor. Daniel learned from her about the insurrections that had swept the land at the beginning of the nineteenth century, the messianic movement headed by a crazy anti-republican religious fanatic who couldn't be defeated – not even by the army.

"There are lots of poems, films, plays and pictures inspired by the Northeast,"Olinda went on.

She went to the kitchen again and came back with a big jug of juice: a blend of orange and papaya. They had spent more than two hours chatting and only now did Daniel mention Luigi. "Look, I'm not sure yet, but I might be sharing the room with my friend, Luigi, he's a nice guy, you'll get along, he's a writer," he explained.

"I'm sure I'll like him if he's your friend."And then she asked, "Is he your boyfriend?"

He laughed. "Oh, no, no! Nothing like that!"It was clear, the question had rattled him; it had never occurred to Daniel that anybody could think of them as homosexuals.

"Well, if the room suits you, it's OK with me."

He lay on his back on the big round straw mat on the floor, propping his head on his hands. Olinda went on, "I was born in Bom Jesus de Lapa, by the river, where the people of the *sertâo* have their religious festivals. Oh, my poor, starving country, the Sâo Francisco is the people's only friend, we all talk about the river as a kind and compassionate relative; we depend so much on it!"She paused, sighed, and then continued, "Away from the river, in the *sertâo*, people suffer; the children eat dirt, to make up for the lack of iron in their diet; they all look ashen, colourless. I was lucky to have been born by the water."

He didn't want Olinda to stop talking. He would have liked her to tell him more about her life, to share her dreams, but he felt exhausted. The last thing he could remember before falling asleep was the image of the woodpecker just outside the window, its bright plumage illuminated by the red evening sun, the elongated bill pecking at the trunk of a tree. Daniel thought, "I can live here for ever."

When he opened his eyes, Olinda was sitting on the floor, one of his feet in her hands. She was applying a gentle massage to his right sole, up and down and up again, stopping in some places, putting pressure on certain spots.

"*Shlof gikher, me darf di kishn.*"

He recognised the language but felt confused; he was still half asleep, doubtful whether he had heard it right; it seemed as if the wrong words were coming out of the wrong mouth. It was difficult to wake up but, in the end, he managed.

"That sounds like Yiddish. Where did you pick that up? You aren't Jewish, are you?"

"I'm not, but my husband was. He was the only child of Holocaust survivors. Did I tell you that he also was a writer? He died of cancer, very young,"she explained, her eyes full of sorrow. He had imagined that Olinda was divorced, or that she had been abandoned by the father of her child, or that her pregnancy had been a youthful mistake. He couldn't have imagined a death in the family.

"Do you know what that saying means? "Sleep faster, I need the pillow."'

The sparkle was back in her eyes; the sadness had dissipated.

"I have no pillow,"he complained jokingly.

When he was a child, his grandmother often told him some of these old sayings. Even when he couldn't fully understand their meaning, he enjoyed the play on words, the surprising and absurd juxtaposition of contrasting situations.

"Whenever my grandmother had to punish me for something I'd done, she would say: *"Don't be silly! Got heyst oykh keyn nar nit zayn!* God never asked anybody to be stupid."'

"How did you know I was Jewish?"Daniel asked her after a while.

"With a name like Goldstein?'

Throughout this conversation, Olinda hadn't stopped massaging his feet. Daniel felt a bit puzzled: although the massage was very sensual, it had not become erotic. He preferred it like that.

"Who is Wanda?"Olinda was looking at him intently. Daniel tried to recall what they had been talking about before he fell asleep; he couldn't remember having mentioned her.

"You kept calling her in your dreams: "Wanda, Wanda, Wanda …""She stood up, the massage session over.

Daniel felt an immediate urge to run out and look for Wanda. He didn't want to talk any more.

"I'd like to have a shower,"he said abruptly. He remembered the offensive stench in the bathroom. It also occurred to him that he didn't have any clothes to change into, everything had gone with the suitcases.

"You can have a shower in the patio, I improvised a system, it's rather primitive, but it works."

She got a towel from some open shelves next to the bathroom and gave it to him. The scent of mothballs comforted him; it reminded him of rainy afternoons in his parents' house, his mother unpacking the family's sweaters and woollen socks from their plastic bags in readiness for winter.

"Here's some soap and shampoo; come on, I'll show you where it is."

A door at the end of the long corridor opened onto a square courtyard. Big pots distributed around the tiled floor were planted with different varieties of thyme: pink, white, mauve. At the end of the patio there was a brick wall, backing on to wilderness. A wooden post stood in the middle, holding the improvised shower: an old metal watering can at the top. It was attached to a movable bracket that could be swung by pulling on a long piece of string; every time one pulled, a trickle of water came down from the spout. A hose strategically positioned along the top of the wall filled the can.

"Will you manage?" Olinda pointed towards the watering can. "Shall I show you how to use it?" She was already holding the string.

"It isn't that complicated," he replied. She stopped and looked at him, realising that she was treating him as a child.

Once she left, he took off his clothes and piled them in a corner of the patio. In spite of the rain it was still hot and humid; sooner or later it would rain again. He liked the heat, although at times it was too oppressive; it made him feel ill, unable to move, too lazy to think. Daniel decided to wash his underpants and his socks. As he was picking them up from the floor, he heard the voice of a woman coming from one of the first floor windows next door: "*Sabado...*" she said.

What about Saturday? What was she referring to? It wasn't going to be easy to have a conversation, naked as he was, with a toothless old woman holding a big *charuto* in her mouth, talking nonsense. Without dropping the cigar, she explained: "The drums, the drums, they're playing the drums tonight, you could visit them tomorrow if you wanted to, they accept visitors on weekends." Then, he heard them. At first, it was a faint faraway sound; as he concentrated, soon the sound coming from the valley filled the space with its vibrations. It was contagious; the rhythm spread all over his body, made his heart beat faster.

"*Tá legal, nâo tá?* – it's OK, isn't it?"the old woman exclaimed.

It was strange to be standing there, holding his underpants and his socks against his genitals in a pathetic attempt to cover them, listening to the people from the *favelas* already preparing for the Carnival, rehearsing their songs and dances.

He decided to ignore his shame, moved back under the watering can, and pulled the string. He quickly washed his clothes and hung them from a couple of big nails in the wall; then he finished washing himself. The old woman didn't expect any reply; she was locked in her own world, and quite happy to be lost in there. He dried himself with the towel, put his jeans back on and a T-shirt borrowed from Olinda. He bade the old woman goodbye.

Going down the hill on the *bondinho*, Daniel wondered where and how he was going to find Luigi. The best thing was to go to Lapa, and hang around the Bar Lua. Daniel knew that Luigi would probably think of doing the same. With a bit of luck, Wanda would be with him.

The tram was empty, nobody was going down to the city at this time of the evening. Daniel sat at the back. He had brought Damián's letter with him to show it to Luigi; he read it once more. Things didn't sound good; the letter confirmed his uneasiness, but it also made him feel vaguely guilty; it was not easy to connect with what was going on in Argentina. While Damián spoke of a possible obsession with death, Daniel felt liberated;

for him, the future -although uncertain- was full of promise, of things to come. Instead, Damián even spoke of an improbable civil war. How could *that* be imagined?

It was nearly eleven when he finally made it to the bar: Saturday night, the place was full to bursting. The noise was loud and the music alternated between bossa nova, which was already becoming part of the Establishment (gone were the days when Joâo Gilberto had shaken people with *Chega de Saudade*) and a new sound, a form of popular music that had been influenced by jazz and rock 'n"roll. Cigarette smoke blended with the smoke from the joints that were passed around.

He ordered a beer at the bar. It took some time for him to get used to the dim light. He glanced around but there was nobody there. After finishing his second beer, he was ready to give up when he saw Luigi at the end of the long corridor, sitting at a table with another guy.

"Where the hell have you been? I've been waiting for you for the last four hours."They hugged, slapping each other on the back, happy.

"I've got a lot to tell you."

"Let's hear it."

"I've lost the suitcases – some punks stole them,"Daniel briefly explained.

"That's funny."

But Luigi wasn't laughing. Instead, he asked, "What else?'

"We have a place to live, it's a room in a big house, in the morro de Santa Teresa, you can even hear the drums from the *favelas*."

"Great! How much?"It wasn't an unreasonable question, but it had never occurred to him to ask.

"No idea, the owner is a painter, her name is Olinda Morais, you'll like her; she comes from the Northeast, she's a communist."

"*Everybody* knows Olinda Morais!"said the stranger sitting at the table.

"Meet Leandro Cabral, he's the director of an orchestra, the IPA, the Ipanema Pro-music Association. They're trying to make it professionally."

"Allow me, please, to buy you a drink,"the man said, and without waiting for an answer he stood up and walked towards the counter.

"Who is this guy?'

"I was here, happy by myself. Then, a while ago, he grabbed a chair, introduced himself, and sat down. All of a sudden, he started pontificating about modern Brazilian music, he has a thing about it. I renamed him el Señor Sotana because he reminds me of one of the priests from the seminary. You've gotta hear him speak, he thinks he's the Pope!'

"Where is Wanda? What did you do after you left?'

"She'll be here soon. We walked around for a while; then she took me to her place. I must confess that I tried to seduce her, but she claims to be in love with you. She talks about you all the time. So you'd better be ready – the writing's on the wall and I foresee a lot of trouble ahead."

"Like what?'

"Oh I don't know, I sensed something, that's all. Did you know she had a pimp?"

"Sort of, but don't lecture me. What on earth could happen to me? No pimp's going to kill me. Here, I want you to read Damián's letter, the situation in Argentina is what really worries me right now. Onganía is a son of a bitch, we've never had somebody like him in power, there is something sinister about this guy."

El Señor Sotana was back with three *chopps*. "I hope this beer is to your liking. Are you also a smuggler like your friend?'

Daniel looked at Luigi, who was smiling. "Did Luigi tell you? This is not something I'd like to have spread around."

El Señor Sotana opened his eyes wide, as if surprised: "Well, you see,"(one could tell he loved saying "you see') "I inspire confidence in people, they know what I'm about, they trust me;

I'm not just the director of an orchestra, I am a communication *artiste*."

A real find.

"I should have guessed it, now that I think about it; you have such ... how shall I put it? Such a papal presence!'

"You see, I have been to Europe, to the Iberian Peninsula, I have learnt about people, I'm a bit of a psychologist, *and* I'm planning to write a novel."

Really.

"My family comes from Europe, you see, I have Portuguese ancestors."

The *cariocas* seemed to hate the Portuguese, claiming that they were all moody, gloomy, and dyspeptic.

Luigi was quicker than Daniel: "You said you were a bit of a psychologist."

"Indeed,"the Big Man responded.

"Daniel and I were arguing about a deep psychological question that has been bothering me for a while. When would you say that, in the context of a marriage, it would be acceptable to start farting in bed? I mean, if one of the spouses farted, willingly and consciously, without making any effort to leave the matrimonial bed while the other spouse was already under the covers, would you consider this to be the end of the romantic period in a relationship, or –alternatively – would you maintain that this is the very beginning of true intimacy?'

The man looked bewildered.

"You see, some people dismiss farts too easily but I consider it an art, it's undoubtedly part of human creativity. Did you know, for example, that at the turn of the century the Moulin Rouge in Paris had as one of its regular artists – among others, like Sarah Bernhardt and Yvette Guilbert – a man called Joseph Pujol, alias *Le Pétomane*?"

"No, I didn't, actually,"said el Señor Sotana, tilting his head.

"He was a miracle, a magician with no tricks. *Le Pétomane*

could attach to his anus a little flute with six stops and play, for example, *Le Roi Dagobert* and *Au claire de la lune."*

Two cold, small hands covered Daniel's eyes from behind. So close to his body, he recognised the smell of that hair, Wanda's unique laugh, her inviting, delectable breath. His heart started to pound.

"Guess who?'

"Whoever you are, Princess of Darkness, you smell good: you're spicy, well-seasoned, I love the aroma of your promises, I'd like a taste of whatever you have to offer. I'd eat you up."

"Jolly good poetry!"el Señor Sotana intervened.

"You could eat me if you wanted to,"Wanda whispered in his ear, "but the question is, can you afford my fees?'

Wanda was more beautiful than he remembered. He contemplated her as she sat on his lap: her velvety skin darkened by the sparse light; her eyes, black fire; the full lips, always half parted; her defiant, cheeky manner. She was wearing a wide, flowery, cotton gypsy skirt, and a white top. Daniel stroked her back, under her shirt. He was bewitched by a certain vulnerability beneath her sensual gestures. He understood well why men would want to buy her favours, but for a split second the thought of what she did for a living sent shivers down his spine. He remembered a reference in Cesare Pavese's *Journal* about his disgust at finding another man's sperm in his lover's body.

People were still arriving at the bar, and very few who were there seemed ready to leave; they had never seen the place so crowded.

"You know,"el Señor Sotana was saying, "I don't understand this young generation. I'm a classical musician, but I can accept other forms of musical expression. In terms of popular music, for example, I'm a man of waltzes, foxtrots, boleros. I can even understand the reasons for people's inclination for tarantellas, fandangos, paso-dobles and the rumba, and – if I'm forced to include that perverse dance on the list – even, the tango. But seriously, to think that they go mad for this rubbish of bossa nova! I deplore their taste."And then, pointing to the speakers on the wall: "Listen to it, it's beyond my comprehension."

"Then this is the last place you should be in,"protested Luigi. El Señor Sotana continued, oblivious. No skin there, only a thick shell. "These musicians prostitute themselves, they willingly sell out to the Yankees, they give away our culture for crumbs, they are worse than whores."

"I believe that a whore would do you good,"Wanda said, agitated. Daniel could feel her back tensing, ready for a fight. The man was taken aback; he obviously couldn't quite understand what he had said wrong.

"And considering you're a musician, you seem to be very ignorant. What do you know about Brazilian music anyway? Do you think that *bossa nova* came out of nothing? There was a tradition: Ismael, Cartola, Noel, those *sambistas da Velha Guarda*, *they* created Gal Costa, Gilberto Gil, Caetano Veloso, Nara Leâo, Tom Zé."

Wanda proceeded to bombard el Señor Sotana with names of composers and titles of songs; she sang fragments of old sambas, and quoted what this or that singer from the Old Guard once said on a TV programme, as if she were fighting for her life. "It's the same music in different forms, the same soul, this is what people really like. Who are you to tell them what they want? Are you also going to tell them not to smoke, not to jerk off, or worse still, that they shouldn't go to whores?'

Daniel secretly wished to prevent men from going to some whores.

After the explosion, el Señor Sotana looked beaten. He retreated, stammering a goodbye, vanishing into the thick smoke that filled the place.

As soon as the Pope left, Luigi too got up and wandered away from their table. With his arms around Wanda, Daniel could feel her relaxing. She stuck her hand in between her breasts and pulled out a joint – long, thin, perfectly formed; she got a light from a guy at the next table and, after puffing away at it, offered it to him. The young man returned it with a smile and passed it to Daniel. He was ready to take a drag when Wanda stopped him. "Wait! Let me help you."

She proceeded to take a deep puff, and then kissed Daniel on the mouth. He let the smoke invade his lungs and felt it reach into his whole body, touching his brain. "What are you wearing? Your perfume is driving me nuts. It has a very attractive smell, pears and apples and roses."

"It's musk. I bought it from a *bahiana* at a street market; she informed me that a Yoruba goddess uses it to attract her lovers. Even animals use it: ducks, lizards, deer, turtles. I specially wanted to attract a certain male from my own species. The *bahiana* told me that once he got a sniff of my scent, he wouldn't be able to go after any other female; he wouldn't ever leave me. I paid a lot for it but I didn't mind, I had made a little money with the *jogo do bicho*."

"What's that?'

"An illegal lottery. Well-brought-up boys like you are not allowed to play – only real men can."

Foolishly, Daniel felt hurt. "Do you make your customers wear condoms?"The truth was coming out, the idiot couldn't control his jealousy.

Wanda pushed away from him brusquely. Her face hardened, the smile disappeared. Maybe, the thought crossed Daniel's mind, Wanda was just too much for him. In part, he would have been relieved if at that moment she had walked out on him. Daniel recovered just in time. He remembered, *"Navegar é preciso/ Viver não é preciso* – To sail is necessary, to live is not."That song helped to restore his courage.

Wanda searched his face: "I've only fucked a client on two separate occasions, and only because I wanted to. I'd had a fight with my lover, it was only revenge. And yes, I made them wear a condom, of course. But anyway, that was a long time ago. Men don't come to me for sex; they want to talk, to be understood, to cry on my shoulder, to be babies again. Most of the times they can't even get it up, and when they do, they barely make it to a wank."

Daniel remembered his own experience with a prostitute, and thought of Luigi's: could it have been so great for him?

Wanda stared at him. Then, she changed her tune: "*Calamidade!* D'you know what my grandmother used to say: "Don't blow your nose, your brains will spill out.""

He burst out laughing and kissed her.

"You know what I would really like to achieve in life?"she went on. "To die for love, I think love is everything, the only thing that makes any sense of this world, I want to die for it."

Wanda. Oh, generous one.

"Sometimes I imagine that my lover is a soldier. He goes far away to fight in a war. After many months I receive news that he has been killed in a heroic battle: he alone, against many enemies. I get very sad, cry and wail and howl in pain. I imagine myself living in a circular room; the bed is right in the middle of it, facing the windows; I lie on it, and let myself die, slowly, like a faithful dog forsaken by its owner; I'll die of *saudade* – of nostalgia."

Wanda. Please.

"Do you know,"Daniel asked suddenly, "that the *blattella germanicae* have been around for 300 million years?'

"What are they?"Wanda asked incredulously.

"Cockroaches, and do you know why they have been on earth for that long? One reason is quite obvious: they just eat any shit they can find; but the main reason is that they fuck a lot; they are always ready for it, and they do it by attracting each other through smell. Every time they feel like it – both, males and females – they can produce this attractive scent to tempt a member of the opposite sex."

"Where did you learn all this?'

"The male produces this substance that she loves to eat; as soon as she starts nibbling on it, he gets multiple erections – multiple erections! Do you hear me? He doesn't have one, he doesn't have two, he has many pricks, but only one is needed to hook into the female's body, and once hooked, they stay hooked, fucking each other silly for hours."

Wanda listened spellbound. "I never thought I would be turned on by a story about cockroaches, wait for me."She got up and disappeared.

Daniel closed his eyes and listened to the music. Above the noise of the crowd he could hear the voice of a woman. The song reminded him of the political and emotional liberation that he and his friends had talked about so often (and dreamt about so vividly) on those long nights in Buenos Aires. Raúl González Tuñón had once said to him, "The only possible revolution is a poetic one'. At that time, while listening to old tangos at the Bar Unión, it had made perfect sense. He wasn't too sure now what "poetic" was, nor was he certain any more what "revolution" meant. Everything was confused in his mind.

Rumours continued to circulate in Rio about the increasing repression. The only certainty was that no revolution was going to be possible for as long as the army was in power. Maybe the only liberation was a spiritual one, away from the masses, far from the crowd.

"I wonder whether something like Confucianism, for instance, would be any good for the working-classes?"And what about the lumpenproletariat? "Could they be helped in any way?"he heard himself asking out loud. He laughed and opened his eyes. Marx hadn't felt much sympathy for marginal characters who didn't contribute to the cause of the workers' revolution.

"And yet," Daniel thought, "I feel quite an affinity with dropouts in general." He didn't care that much for production; after all, poets didn't produce anything at all, they should be considered part of a certain enlightened lumpenproletariat. The maconha was making him think some very stupid things. Didn't Confucius propose celibacy? Nobody in their right mind would accept it. Could any theory of liberation exclude sex? Tantric yoga might be the right thing, yes!, a sacred and mystical union with God. By making love to a woman, one would be consorting with the Divine; sex was the only religious practice, the real purpose of being. The more sex, the greater the divine joy. If there were any truth, it lived in the body and was attained by fucking. What about a Tantric Party for Erotic Socialism in Latin America? He had to write to Damián about this possibility. A wonderful voice came through the speakers. Daniel wished his native tongue was Brazilian Portuguese: a language with style, movement, and swing; it had a rhythm that just by itself created some kind of poetic reminiscence. It had humour and irony; it made the body sing and forced the soul to dance. Maybe it was invented by a Tantric yogi! During his visit to Congonhas, he had seen a Yank posing as an Indian fakir, scrawny and turbaned, lying on a bed of nails in a Sunday street market. Surrounded by so many hungry and emaciated people, he didn't look out of place. On the contrary, he fitted in well among the oranges and pineapples and live chickens, waiting on his uncomfortable bed for the few coins that never materialised, ignored by the passing crowd. Daniel had stood for some time looking at the fake yogi lying there like a corpse, under a big black umbrella that protected him from the hot morning sun. At one point, another guy arrived on the scene: blond, beefy and tanned, smoking a cigarette. The yogi got up and started cheerfully chatting to his friend, who tied a big leather belt around the bed of nails and lifted it onto his shoulders; then, the two of them walked off, happily laughing and making jokes in their American twang.

Where had Wanda gone?

There was quite a difference, he went on laughing to himself, between a yogi on a bed of nails and a woman lying on a bed. Maybe it was a male obsession, this fascination with the image of a female body, asleep, abandoned, tranquil, sexually inviting. He always found it a turn-on to look at his partner naked, half covered by the sheets, her hair untidy. Was it ever the same for a woman looking at a man? The image of a sleeping woman was an erotic delight. But why? Was it the pleasure given by the illusion that one could have total dominance over a woman?

Somebody was singing *Antonico*. "It's the same soul,"Wanda had said. She was right: this was one perfect example of a young singer paying tribute to an old composer from another generation. Black African slaves were responsible for this wonderful music. The slaves in Argentina had also been persecuted by their masters for their drums and weird religious practices. In Buenos Aires, their dances were called *tambo*, and the most important was *el candombe*. Like the *escolas de samba* in Rio, Buenos Aires had its *candombe* groups at the turn of the century: *Conga, Angola, Benguela, Lubolos, Mina, Cabunda*. They sang: *A-eeé!... A-eeé!/ Calunga mishinga/Mishinga-eeé!* They were secret, sensual, defiant; they were all created around el Barrio del Tambor –later renamed San Telmo. Anything to erase the traces of slavery in Argentina.

He saw Wanda moving slowly through the crowd; he thought – in a ridiculous association – that she looked like Kim Novak in *Picnic*, with her pink skirt and blond hair, walking across the bridge to meet William Holden. It seemed to take ages for her to push through the crowd and arrive at their table. She stood by his side, still moving, dancing, mouthing the lyrics of *Antonico*; she opened her lips provocatively, showed her tongue, closed her eyes. At times, her long curly hair covered her face and she tossed her head. He wanted to embrace her but he didn't move, just stayed still in his chair, looking at her, desiring her, making her want him. Like Marlon Brando, he imagined. Then, she sat on top of him as if she were riding a horse, lifting her gypsy skirt to make it easier to straddle him. He could smell not only the musk from the Yoruba goddess, but this time he could sense the combination of sweet and strong aromas that made men go wild. They embraced and kissed. He caressed her back, and pressed her to him, anticipating that it was going to be difficult to stop.

Against his better judgement, he slid one of his hands under the light fabric of her skirt and pulled it to cover his lap. She had no underwear on; had she gone to take it off? He undid the button of his jeans and wiggled to get the zipper down. Wanda moved on top of him ably, with such elegance and ease that he entered her almost instantly with no apparent effort. Daniel remained motionless, wrapped in her arms, his head against the soft, smooth breasts. She never stopped moving her body, gently, just enough, swaying to the music. He felt held by her, suspended in the air in defiance of gravity, all the pleasure of this world concentrated for an instant between those two bodies. After all that waiting, it happened all too quickly. She laughed and kissed him again and clutched his head, saying, "you owe me one."

Little Brown Sugar.

As he opened his eyes he could see over her shoulders, across the long room, a group of policemen charging through the door.

PART II

1

It wasn't clear who had made the decision but Wanda, Luigi and Daniel all moved in at the same time into Olinda's. The flat-fronted colonial house, which Olinda had been renting for many years, had more than enough space. The front door opened directly to a huge living room, with wooden floors and blue and yellow Portuguese tiles halfway up the whitewashed walls. To the right of the entrance, an old leather sofa and assorted cane chairs, together with cushions covered in Indian cotton on the floor were arranged around a low painted wooden table. On the other side, a small round table with untidy heaps of books, a telephone, and piles of dog-eared, out-of-date directories stood in the corner next to the hi-fi; long-play records were strewn everywhere. Further back, a dining table capable of seating up to twelve people, was near the door to the kitchen. At the end of the living room, an archway led to the stairs to the upper floor, and to a corridor with a doorway to the patio. The troubled bathroom was beneath the stairs.

Olinda and Wanda soon discovered that they shared an interest in *umbanda*, a kind of white magic that was very popular in Rio, a mixture of *candomblé* and spiritualism. The two women spent hours comparing notes on their experiences with different *pais de santo*. Wanda told Olinda of countless migraines that had been cured by her *pai*, while Olinda reported cures of rheumatic fever, peptic ulcers, all sorts of poisoning, and even a case of syphilis. Wanda listened intently to Olinda's stories, full of admiration for the undeniable powers of such a wonderful man.

Olinda had sent her son to stay with her parents, who still lived in Bom Jesus de Lapa. "I want David to learn everything there is to know about the Sâo Francisco – that river was the most important influence in my life. Inspired by the river, my son could become a great man, like Jorge Amado or Einstein."

Very soon, Olinda and Luigi began an intense and inevitable love affair. One evening, they started holding hands during dinner. It seemed only natural.

Luigi was working on a science-fiction novel, which told – in allegorical form – the story of his family. He spent long hours at the typewriter, an old Royal in mint condition that Olinda borrowed for him from a neighbour. It was immaculate: small glass panels on the sides and a jumpy but remarkably shiny steel return lever. Every day, before Luigi started work, Olinda wiped the lever, glass panels and keys with a soft piece of chamois leather and liquid polish. Then they went for a walk. When they got back, while Luigi clacked at the keys of the Royal, Olinda worked on her paintings. Images of the *sertâo* had been replaced by more overtly political themes: union leaders killed by soldiers, student demonstrations, police interrogations.

Wanda listened in silence to long discussions about the peasant rebellions in Peru, the Pope's ruling on contraception, the contrast between revolutionary Catholic priests in other countries and the reactionary Church in Brazil, the chronic stupidity of the Communist Party's opportunistic policies. Daniel's great passion was the Catalan anarchist movement during the time of the Spanish Republic. He would conclude discussions with the same gloomy statement, "All political parties are shit."

One day Wanda appeared with a poster of Ché Guevara, which she hung in their room, opposite their bed. "I'm not sure who he is but I just love his beard ... *and* one more thing: I've given up my job,"she announced. There was no further discussion. Daniel wanted to write a series of long poems around the image of "a woman asleep', but felt stuck. On the few occasions that he contemplated Wanda sleeping, he felt inspired – but only rarely did the images became poems. He spent most of his time reading and re-reading *20 Poemas de Amor y una Canción Desesperada*:

> *I like it when you're silent*
> *as if you were absent...*

The day they had moved in, the plumbing system stopped playing jokes on them. Olinda was convinced that this had something to do with Wanda's presence. Wanda spoke of Olinda's house as the first home she'd ever had. She had never felt so comfortable, so at ease. They spent many hours together, talking and giggling, doing each other's hair, and swapping clothes like adolescent girls.

Olinda wanted to paint the house; she needed a change, a break with the past. The two women went out and bought the paint: two different shades of yellow, a sky blue, a brilliant orange. They also got brushes, sandpaper, and filler for the cracks in the walls. In two hectic weekends, the four of them completely transformed the place. Not only did they paint the walls, they also cleaned the cupboards, rearranged the furniture, and got rid of all sorts of rubbish that Olinda had collected over the years.

A new addition to the family was a bird that Olinda's mother-in-law brought one day to the house: a red-fan parrot that had travelled on the woman's right shoulder all the way from Visconde de Itabapoana, a place up in the mountains west of Rio, where she ran Brazil's first vegetarian restaurant. "He, or she – we've never known – has gone wild since my husband's death, the bird attacks all my customers; it's jealous of the goat, terrorising the poor animal; it shits in the cooking pots in the kitchen, especially on the brown rice. Either I get rid of him, or her, or I'll end up killing him, or her…'

Olinda was reluctant to accept the bird, but felt unable to refuse. She loved and admired her mother-in-law. She had spent many happy times at her house – a cosy chalet typical of the region. It was ironic that these Holocaust survivors, who had spoken Yiddish for most of their lives and never reneged on their Judaism, should have ended up living in a mountain region settled by German exiles and German-speaking Swiss.

Since the old couple didn't know the sex of the bird, the poor parrot was never even given a name. Wanda thought that this was too cruel: "Everyone needs a name; otherwise, how can God recognise you when you die?'

So off they went with the bird to the local vet, who explained that both sexes of this species had the same colouring, making it difficult to tell them apart. The upper parts were green, the tail, dark blue, the top and sides of the head brown with whitish streaks, and the forehead a dirty white. The most striking characteristic was the nape, which bore a crest of long, dark red, blue-edged feathers extending to the underparts. "You'll be able to tell any change of weather in advance,"the vet told them. "They shriek in a loud and continuous "*iá-iá, iá-iá*". It'll drive you nuts."Finally, proffering the bill for his professional services, he solemnly declared, "It's a boy."

Olinda baptised him Joaquim María, after the famous Brazilian writer Machado de Assis. Luigi and Daniel objected, since the name perpetuated the ambiguity of his sexual identity, but Olinda remained adamant: Joaquim María it would be. Olinda and Wanda were both very happy that the bird was male. Anyhow, sexual ambiguity was not a great source of worry for them.

"We get along better with men,"Wanda joked. But the innocent bird fell for Luigi, followed him everywhere and perched on his shoulder most of the time, raising his crest whenever anybody approached. Joaquim María spent a lot of time grooming Luigi's hair, his beard and, especially, picking his teeth. While Luigi was pounding away at the typewriter, the bird sat on top of the desk keeping watch, making contented conversational sounds. If anybody approached Luigi, he shrieked very loudly.

The parrot's passionate devotion to him provoked terrible quarrels between Olinda and Luigi. She was very jealous and dropped the "Joaquim'; for her, it became only "María'. This in turn rather upset Luigi, who protested vehemently, "This bird is no queer!"To no avail. From then on, he refused to use "María'; as far as he was concerned, the parrot's name was now simply "Joaquim'. After a while, Wanda re-baptised the bird with a composite name: she took "Joaq"and "aria', and turned it into Joacaría, which they all agreed suited the parrot well.

One day he fell from his perch on the windowsill next to the desk while asleep and –inexplicably – twisted and broke one of his legs, after getting himself entangled amongst the keys of the typewriter. This was a tragedy in the otherwise peaceful home. The injury was so bad that the leg had to be amputated and replaced by a wooden one. Joacaría recovered quickly from his loss and was soon racing along the corridor of the flat. In order to avoid complaints from Olinda during her siesta, Luigi stuck a rubber stopper at the tip of the wooden leg to mute the tapping of the wood on the tiles.

Although this type of parrot was not known to be able to talk, there was one phrase in Yiddish that Joacaría had mastered. It had been taught to the bird by Olinda's father-in-law. Everybody in the flat knew when it was sunrise, because the parrot would run up and down the corridor shouting: "Kish me in tochis! Kish me in tochis! –Kiss my ass!'

Santa Teresa, one of Rio's oldest suburbs, suffered from frequent power cuts. Two or three times a week the narrow, twisting tree-lined streets of that beautiful neighbourhood were left in the dark. It always happened, of course, when electricity was most needed. Then, candles and lanterns glowed through the open windows, creating a magical, fairy-tale atmosphere. With no television sets or radios blaring into the night, one was able to hear the noises coming from the jungle. And on Fridays and Saturdays, the drums.

Her parents-in-law had given Olinda a unique gift. It was a silver Chanukah menorah, perhaps from the eighteenth century, with an eight-branched candelabrum and a beautiful ninth candleholder, the *shamash*. Her father-in-law had buried it in the woods near his village before he was taken to the concentration camp. After the liberation, he insisted on going back to the spot to retrieve it. It was in fact his sole possession when he arrived in Brazil. Once he reached the new promised land, he got a job very quickly and never had to sell it, for which he remained forever grateful to his God. Then, it was Olinda's turn to keep it in a closet for years, wrapped in tissue paper and a wool cloth. Now she dared to take it out and use it on the days of the power cuts – only because of the two men in the house, as if she wanted to believe that their reassuring presence would magically eliminate any possibility of theft. The value of this historical piece, she rightly thought, was incalculable.

A box of books had arrived for Daniel at the Consulate; some of them had been hidden by Damián after the shootout at the book launch; the rest came from his parents' house. Now, during those late, dark evenings, Luigi and Daniel took turns reciting their favourite poems while the women listened in the candlelight. Usually, they remained silent after each poem, passing around a bottle of cheap wine from Rio Grande do Sul. Finally, one of them would break the silence with a comment, which sometimes triggered heated arguments, spiked with humor.

As with their political discussions, Wanda didn't participate much at first but, in time, she gained more confidence. She

had her favourites: the Portuguese version of George Brassens'
lyrics (they were available in a mimeographed pirate edition
that Luigi had borrowed from a French artist), and the few
young Russian poets they read in Spanish under the soft light.
Wanda asked them to read Yevtushenko's *Babii Yar* many
times:

Today I seem to be a Jew...

They all agreed to make Mondays and Tuesdays their days of
rest; nobody did any work then. On Mondays they took turns,
usually in pairs, to do a big shop for the coming week; whoever
stayed behind cleaned the house. Whenever it was the women's
turn, Wanda bought all sorts of herbs, spices and flowers from
the open markets, and taught the others the use of plants for
healing that she had learnt from her father.

Vanilla, which helped to clear the nose and throat, was good for
colds and catarrh; her father used to make anyone in the family
who caught a cold sit with their feet in a vanilla bath. Wine made
from certain flowers and berries that only Wanda could spot at
the open-air markets was another panacea for colds. For cuts,
she recommended chewing the stalks of mallow, and applying a
mixture of the pulp and saliva to the wound. When in pain from
unrequited love, wormwood was the main ingredient for a love
charm that should only be used in moderation. Wanda knew of
many friends who had used it unwisely, causing their lovers to
have hallucinations – on a few occasions driving them mad; she
even knew of somebody who had died of it.

When passion needed to be set alight once again, vervain was
used as an aphrodisiac. The situation could also be improved by
a diet that included red peppers and lots of cinnamon, clove and
coriander. And if lack of desire was accompanied by infertility, there
were very few things that worked as well as peppermint, which
was also good for indigestion and headaches. Some medicine men

used marjoram to help reach the souls of the sick. Wanda had heard that, if taken in the right doses, one would see everything blue. To ward off evil spirits, it was best to plant basil around the house, which could also be used as an antiseptic. To paralyse an enemy, deadly nightshade was the thing. And for a witch who needed to fly across the dark skies, the brew was monkshood. Dill was good for the liver, and sesame was recommended for dementia.

Daniel listened in awe, drawn to Wanda's past; he felt curious about her strange family, their religion, their knowledge of plants accumulated for generations. Luigi was quite cynical about their medicinal properties; this made Olinda angry, while Wanda simply ignored him and never took offence.

"You can't stand anyone knowing something you don't know,"complained Olinda.

"I don't think that's the reason at all, I just happen to believe that it's all in the head; if you don't believe in it, it won't work. This is fact: it only works in certain cultures, for certain people, it isn't a universal thing … *Ajonjolí* for madness? Ha! That's crazy."

"You're such an ignorant brute, a true quadruped."

Those two found many reasons to fight but reconciliation was, in the end, a sweet prize. Luigi would get on all fours like an animal, and squeal: "I'm a quadruped, I'm a quadruped…"Olinda pretended to pull him along on an imaginary leash, leading him to different corners of the living-room, admonishing him, warning him to behave like a properly trained pet. Wanda loved the game, and encouraged Olinda with shouts of "Bravo! Bravo!"

Life was perfect.

Daniel couldn't understand how most people in this world could survive without literature. This thought made him feel like a snob, an elitist. But poetry and art were so much part of his and his friends' lives that to exist without them was unthinkable; poetry was what made them stay alive. In his heart, he acknowledged to himself (with pain but no regret) that he was no great poet – nor was he ever going to become one. And yet, in order to go on living, and certainly to continue writing, he needed to believe that he was capable of producing something special, truly unique. Sometimes he wished he could give up literature altogether for something completely different: maybe he'd end up selling silk ties in the markets of Sâo Paulo, driving a taxi in Buenos Aires, or opening a stall by the banks of the River Plate and sell *chorizo* sandwiches. Other poets had done it.

Luigi interrupted his train of thought: "How come you don't read the papers any more? Have you got the blues or something?"he asked. Olinda and Wanda had gone out; they were enjoying a prolonged, lazy breakfast. Daniel, studying the notes to a John Coltrane record that he had just bought; Luigi, reading the *Jornal do Brasil*.

"They depress me too much. I wonder if it makes any real difference to keep in touch with what's going on. Did you know Fabián Bigio in Buenos Aires? He saved a copy of *La Prensa* every day for a whole year without touching it; then, he started reading a copy a day. A twelve-month delay! He claimed it was all the same shit."

"I knew someone who only read the classified ads because it was the only way to really know what was going on. According to him, the news gives people a false sense of reality. But he couldn't escape his destiny: he ended up in a madhouse, where part of the treatment was to read out the news in a group every morning."

Daniel got up, walked towards the hi-fi system, and put on the Coltrane.

"It's a bit early for that kind of heavy stuff, don't you think?"Luigi asked.

The Legend started blowing. *Summertime*, then *My Favourite Things* and later, *Every Time We Say Goodbye*.

"I hear he's given up the sax for religion."

"He had a spiritual crisis, an awakening in which he rediscovered God. His music just went gloriously wild; it made him happier and more productive. The truth is, I wouldn't mind something like that happening to me, it wouldn't matter what: opium, religion, madness, love, or *maconha*. If it transforms your art, wouldn't you take anything?'

"Opium would make more sense than religion ..."Luigi started saying, but suddenly stopped. He was transfixed by the back pages of the *Jornal*. His face had turned white as milk; he whispered, "sons of bitches!'

Daniel moved closer to read the paper over Luigi's shoulder. A small photograph caught his eye: he recognised Eugenio, someone he had known for years, smiling stupidly, in a typical passport shot from a few years back. The stark headlines "Decapitated by Thieves' sent an icy chill down Daniel's spine; his legs felt rubbery, and he felt sick. Nevertheless, he managed to move across the living room and stopped the music. Luigi read the article aloud: a young Argentinian, Eugenio Paredes, who lived on the Ilha de Paquetá, had been murdered by a gang of thieves from Rio. The police suspected three youths who had been spotted on the ferry on a return trip from the island; the public was asked for any information that could help to identify them. The criminals had probably managed to steal very little money; the authorities speculated that, out of frustration, they had also killed a goat and two chickens that Mr Paredes kept in his backyard. The animals had had their throats cut. The police could not explain why the animals had also been slit open: their hearts had been removed and were later found buried in the backyard of his humble house. A long carved wooden pole, stained with the blood of the animals, had been used as part of a cross stuck in the ground. The machete used by the thieves was found lying next to Eugenio's decapitated body.

Eugenio was a writer from Tilcara, in Jujuy. He had been in his early thirties when he had arrived in Buenos Aires with fifteen hundred poems and four novels in his satchel. Every so often he would invite a few friends to his room in a boarding house, offer them pizza and *fainá, empanadas* and wine, a small party. When everybody was drunk he'd taken them to the local square, where he would proceed to light a bonfire and burn one of his manuscripts. Eugenio had invited Daniel to participate in this cruel ritual for his fifth and last novel, written in Buenos Aires.

"Hell! Why? Who would have wanted to murder him?'

They had met him recently at the Argentinian Consulate, collecting his letters. Eugenio had told them that he'd gotten mixed up with *a macumba.* He though that Exú was trying to set up a special order in the world, that he had chosen Eugenio to be his special messenger. So Eugenio had become a member of the Irmandade do Bom Demônio –the Fraternity of the Good Devil, a secret society from the Reconcavo.

"Well,"said Luigi, "that's another one gone, did you know that Eugenio's father was a gravedigger? If your father is socialising with the spirits of the departed, what chance do you have in life?"

"Could it have been a ritual killing? Poor Eugenio, he was trying to learn Yoruba to be able to communicate with the dead."

"He won't need it now,"Luigi said with sadness. After the initial shock, Daniel now felt distant and numb.

"He burnt all those manuscripts, thousands and thousands of words just blown away in smoke; he didn't leave anything behind, nothing!'

Eugenio had never been married, nor did he have any children; even though he had written so much, he hadn't published any of his work. A passport photograph in a *carioca* morning paper was his sole claim to posterity. And a hole in the ground in some forsaken municipal cemetery.

"I wonder if he was made to suffer; maybe the poor bastard was tortured,"said Luigi.

"Perhaps I should go to the police,"ventured Daniel. "After all, they're asking for information."

"They specifically want to know about those three guys, what could you tell them?'

"In these cases, details turn out to be important clues, maybe I can give them some information that might be of help."

He thought he would go to the local police station to make a statement. Eugenio's dealings with the *macumba*, his obsession with Exú, the secret *candomblé* society.

"What puzzles me is the killing of his animals. What did the poor beasts have to do with it?"asked Luigi.

"Who gives a fuck about a pathetic goat and two famished chickens, you seem to be more concerned about the animals than him."

After a pause, Luigi said calmly:

"Animals are more reliable, they never betray you, wouldn't inform on you, sell you out, or let you down."

"I know."His anger was not directed at Luigi.

At that point, Joacaría came limping along the corridor, repeating his limited vocabulary: "*Kish me in tochis! Kish me in tochis!*"He flew first to the sofa's armrest, then hopped quickly onto Luigi's shoulder. He offered the bird his head, for the parrot to groom his curly hair.

"Look at this,"said Luigi, tenderly.

"I'm looking, I'm looking."

"Do you know that these parrots are strictly monogamous? They can live for seventy years, never changing mates, and when they are domesticated they become just like their owners: when I take a bath, Joacaría takes a bath with me; if I sing, he sings; if I shout, he raises his voice. He defends me against all enemies."

"How can you speak like that about a bird full of fleas? Someone we knew has just been beheaded."

"He has no fleas! Besides, life is what counts, not death,"And then he recited: ""*La muerte no sirve para nada...* - Death is no use..." Do you remember *Zorba the Greek*?'

The film had reawakened in them a romantic vision of Greece, something they had first acquired from reading Henry Miller's *The Colossus of Maroussi*.

"When Zorba's old lover dies, he doesn't cry; he just grabs this big cage with a bird that belonged to her, and walks away with it; when he reaches the street, he covers the cage to protect the bird from the sun; he chooses to protect life rather than cry over death."

Daniel was still trying to work out how they had managed to move from talking about Eugenio's murder to Anthony Quinn and his Greek bird, when they heard Olinda and Wanda coming in. They had arrived with their shopping.

"What's going on?"Olinda said, seeing them looking stricken.

They all sat around the table, and Daniel told them about Eugenio. With the bits of information they had, they tried to put the story together, to throw some light on the horrible and seemingly senseless killing.

"I think you should go to the police,"Olinda told him, "I'll come with you."

"No, it's OK, I'll go,"Wanda intervened.

Daniel fetched his shoulder bag and made sure that he had his passport and some money in it. "It's OK for you to come with me, but I don't want you to go inside. Just wait for me somewhere nearby."

"All right,"Wanda accepted.

In truth, there was no reason for Daniel to be concerned about her; she could protect herself very well. It was irrational, he had remained worried about her after the raid in the Bar Lua. In fact, it hadn't gone badly for them: by the time the heavily armed men reached the table where they were sitting, Wanda and Daniel had managed to stand up and smooth down their clothes – despite their recent passionate encounter. When they had been bodily searched, he was scared; he thought they might guess what they had been doing, and pulled them in for offending public morality.

But the police were trained to smell reds under the bed, not the leftover fragrance of lovemaking. And marihuana didn't concern them. In the end, the pigs had arrested a few guys, most probably innocent – all of them students with beards.

At the police station, they weren't at all interested in what he knew about Eugenio. A bored-looking young officer slowly typed up his statement. Daniel signed it, left his telephone number, and was coldly dismissed.

"We'll see what we can do,"the officer said. "We're fighting a war, you know, no time for minor crimes."Daniel felt like punching him.

"I hope the good guys win,"he said. The cop shot him a suspicious look.

They didn't say much to each other on the way up on the *bonde*. She broke the silence: "I have something to tell you."

He looked at her; a breach was unexpectedly opening between them.

"There is this man…"He instantly found himself making alternative plans for the future, all in the space of a few seconds. To escape from this, he thought, *"Memory held us, wild and loving…"*It was inspired by something, but where did it come from?

"… he was a French guy, I think from the Consulate or Embassy,"Wanda continued.

""There *is* this man…""thought Daniel, "but "he *was* a French guy…""

"He used to come to me once a week, always at the same time. He took me in his car to a little hotel in the city. He had a little rucksack with a kettle, a teapot, and a pair of cups and saucers. When we got to the room, he heated water and made tea. We sat by the window, sipping tea and eating chocolate *éclairs* while he told me stories about his unfaithful wife. At first, he gave me the creeps, but he was OK, he paid me a lot of money, I didn't need to do any other work for a while."

Wanda could not look in his eyes. "The first time," she continued, "I thought he might have leather straps or kinky things like that in his bag, but I just took the risk. He asked me if I knew anything about France and I said no; the last time he brought me an LP with songs by Georges Brassens."

"We can finally listen to him!" Daniel said. Wanda had kept the record all this time, obviously knowing they all would have loved to listen to it; she had been too embarrassed to produce it before.

Wanda leaned against his shoulder. He put his arm around her and pressed her against him. Behind her tough pose there was a frightened little girl, dreaming of better times: a husband and a home, kids and security, the respect of others. Living at Olinda's place was the nearest thing to a "normal" life.

Daniel asked her: "What can I do for you?" She shook her head. The *bondinho* was getting closer to their stop. She held his hand and kissed it.

"Actually," she said after a while in a rather formal way, "there is one thing I would like you to do."

"What?'

"Teach me French," she implored.

Of all the possible things Wanda could have asked him for, this was the most deliciously absurd: Daniel didn't know enough French to teach a parrot.

From the *bonde* they walked back to the house at a leisurely pace, taking their time to enjoy lingering kisses under the trees. Wanda heard about Lola for the first time while Daniel learned about Wanda's "horrors'. She was constantly invaded by fantasies that made her live in a dreadful world of fears and anxiety: she was going to be run over by a car and left paralysed; her father, whom she still very much loved and admired, would be bitten by a poisonous snake in the jungle; or Daniel would be attacked with a knife by a violent drunk in an empty street. The fantasies were many and varied; they upset her and made her feel helpless. The images took on an immediate graphic presence in her mind.

"Everybody has those fantasies,"he reassured her. "It's your imagination, it's what makes people creative."

"I don't create anything,"she protested.

"You never know, you might be the best yet-to-be-discovered samba songwriter."This idea seemed to cheer her up a little.

At the last corner, before turning toward the house, Wanda said under her breath: "I have something else to tell you."

"As long as it's no more of your horrors."

"Olinda told me a secret, I don't know if I should tell you."

"If it's a secret, don't tell me."

Nevertheless, further down the road Daniel asked her, full of curiosity, "So? Are you going to tell me this secret?'

"It's about Luigi ... Luigi and a dog,"she confessed. She had been savouring this moment in anticipation. "Apparently when he was a child, he had this thing going with a bitch that belonged to one of his neighbours."

"What thing? Ridiculous! With a bitch?"But he was hooked. "What kind of bitch?'

"A bitch called Ágata."

"I don't believe a word of it,"Daniel laughed.

"It belonged to a lady who lived next door; he told Olinda that he used to go every afternoon in the summer and play in her backyard; he sat under a tree during those long school holidays, opened his fly, pulled out his prick, and let Ágata lick it."

He imagined Luigi with his legs open, wanking away with a dog under the shade of a tree. It was hilarious. "Well, it's not much of a love affair, is it?"he said laughing.

As they were opening the door of the flat, Wanda asked, "you won't tell him, promise?'

"Of course not! What's the worry anyway?'

They found Luigi in the living room, making some notes, Joacaría perched on his shoulder, grooming his hair. Olinda was probably having a siesta.

"How did it go?"Luigi asked.

Wanda disappeared into the kitchen. They could hear her singing to herself. After a while, Luigi demanded, "What's wrong?"After hesitating a few seconds, Daniel came out with it: "I know about Ágata."

They both collapsed in laughter.

"I told you, one shouldn't trust human beings, they always betray your secrets."

"Such a smart ass, you son of a bitch."

Luigi told him about the summers in his neighbour's backyard, how it had all started. He was ten years old, and lived in fear of being caught; the owner of the dog was a fat woman called Claudia who lived with her brother.

Olinda, still half asleep, stumbled through the door and in passing she lovingly stroked Luigi's hair. Wanda appeared with the precious LP and put it on.

It was evident, that deep voice moved her.

From then on, they listened to Brassens all the time, morning, noon and night. Joacaría soon dropped his Yiddish and picked up a few French words: *première arète* became his favourite early morning greeting, closely followed by *tramontane*; *Valéry* occupied a comfortable third place. Olinda thought that Joacaría used words to express changes in her mood, and talked to the bird in different tones of voice according to her own feelings. Wanda tried to learn the songs, while Daniel suffered in silence his inability to speak the language.

"Here you have it,"Luigi said emphatically, "a living symbol of the destiny of your race."

"What are you talking about?'

"Assimilation, that's what I'm talking about, even a parrot raised as a Jew would like to become a Gentile."

"Not all Jews want to assimilate."

"Not all of them, but enough of them,"Luigi insisted.

"If you were persecuted for thousands of years, you too might want to identify with your enemy, become strong and powerful."

A particularly sour point. In Argentina, anti-Semitism was everywhere, though everyone denied it. Daniel had been in frequent street fights against the ultra-nationalists – especially during the bitter campaign against compulsory Catholic instruction in state schools. He must have been fourteen then, and carried a cosh in his school bag. This had given him some reassurance, although he was aware that a piece of hosepipe full of gravel and sand was completely useless against the guns and knives his enemies used.

"But look at Joacaría,"added Daniel, "it's true, he lost the little Yiddish he knew, but he didn't learn Portuguese or Spanish, which would have been the most logical thing to do; he picked up French instead. He's still keeping himself a bit of an outsider."

There was one image that Daniel could not erase from his mind: he kept on seeing, as he had seen many times from the windows of buses and trams, the walls of Buenos Aires covered with graffiti urging: "Be a patriot! Kill a Jew!"

2

Daniel, my dear friend,

Thanks for your letter, the articles from the paper, and the wonderful book. Yes, I declare my ignorance: I hadn't heard of Carlos Drummond de Andrade, isn't that shameful? I try (tiredness allowing) to read a few poems out loud from the book every night, before falling asleep. Laura makes fun of my Portuguese accent. It sounds strange to hear ourselves laughing. Nowadays, given what's happening around here, we have to content ourselves with whatever bits of pleasure we can muster. I have stopped writing for the time being, but of course I go on with my teaching.

Two colleagues from the Teachers' Union have been jailed; they were members of the CP, like myself. As you well know, the CP is pretty harmless. The Central Committee is more worried about what Moscow thinks, and about being accepted by the bourgeoisie; the revolution is not an urgent priority. But the malignant propaganda spread through the media, sympathetic to the government, warning the Argentinian people of an imaginary communist, atheist, Jewish, anti-Christian and anti-Western plot, is succeeding in creating a state of terror. We're witnesses to the triumph of barbarism. That sense of minimal personal security that we used to have in this city has been deteriorating fast. The uncertainty started the very night they invaded the Faculty of Exact Sciences; since then, it has been just getting worse. The guys in government have a sinister messianic belief that they are here to save us; this is the most dangerous thing, it creates fanatics.

I'm sorry to be so gloomy, not everything is bad news. Bob Kennedy's strong protest to Lyndon Johnson made Onganía send a letter expressing good will to the Jewish community; he now seems concerned (perhaps due to Yankee pressure) to present an image of "democracy" to the outside world. Nevertheless, who would trust such "gestures"? Anyway, things are all OK in the family: Laura is well and is looking as beautiful as ever, and the kids seem very happy. I'd like to end this with Drummond's verses: Mundo mundo vasto mundo,/if my name were Raimundo/ it would be a rhyme, not a solution. Chau. Say hi! to Luigi and a big hug for you.

Your friend,
Damián

3

Sometimes, Daniel felt that if he didn't write, it was only because he didn't have much to say. This was a feeling which often haunted him – and yet, it remained ambiguous. It was that very ambiguity which, ironically, motivated him to write. He dreamt of a time in which he would convert his writing into a cathartic activity, an act of total liberation, where the past would be confused with the present, where all the different characters and situations that were once part of his life would come together in one single instant of realisation. Consciousness would not be necessary; the destiny of such writing could not be defined, it would neither explain nor justify anything.

And one day, naturally, spontaneously, Daniel locked himself in their bedroom and wrote for three consecutive days and nights. He did it with rage, with nostalgia, as if this were his last creative gesture. He didn't eat much – an occasional cup of coffee, perhaps a sandwich. He hardly moved away from the desk, apart from maybe a short walk and a quick shower. It had never happened to him before. Wanda understood and left him alone. He felt possessed, mad, but happy.

When he woke up from his poetic trance, he realised that the signs had been there for all to see. And yet, they had remained blind to them. First, the fresh milk kept going sour and the cheese went mouldy. They thought the fridge might not be working properly, but the repairman – who charged a fortune for his visit – gave it a clean bill of health. Then, one of the pots of thyme in the patio wilted and died – this happened overnight. Wanda thought that it might have been the neighbourhood cats pissing in the pots. No one agreed. Why would cats choose such unlikely places when they had the entire jungle to piss and shit in at their leisure? Then there were Wanda's nightmares, which tormented her and made her cry; day after day she awoke to recount them to Daniel over breakfast.

Only later, when remembering these events, did they give them due importance; they saw them as a bad omen. A case of the future shaping the past.

Nevertheless, there were two things that couldn't pass unnoticed: first, water started shooting up the sinkholes again. Olinda woke Wanda up to show her the muck coming up the pipes; she pleaded desperately for Wanda to do something about it. What could she do? Thankfully, the strange event only lasted a couple of hours, long enough though to lower everybody's spirits.

Then, they noticed Joacaría's silence: he had gone completely mute, distant, and sunk into a melancholic stupor. Luigi spent part of the morning sitting with him by the window, talking to him, reciting love poems in Italian, telling the bird some of the most beautiful stories he could recall. To no avail.

In the afternoon, when Daniel (who was feeling especially happy after having accomplished his feat of poetic catharsis) opened the front door and saw the monkeys standing there, he knew instantly: the Angels of Death had arrived.

"We should have nailed the skin of an owl to this door," he said by way of greeting.

"What does that mean?"asked one of the men. Tall and fat, he could have been the strong man from the circus – except for his crewcut, which gave him away as a policeman.

"The skin of an owl on a door protects decent homes from any form of evil."Daniel smiled broadly while speaking to them. "It's just a joke, gentlemen. How can I help you? If it's insurance you're selling, we don't need any."

"Police,"said the strong man, who seemed to be the leader. "We've come to search the house."No formal introductions.

"Do you have a warrant?"This was amusing; he was aware that they couldn't give a fuck about legal procedures.

The apes looked at each other, sidelong. "Is this enough of a warrant?"asked the leader, opening his jacket just enough to show a gun lying over his heart.

"We don't have anything to hide, this house will always welcome people like you."The gun was surely loaded, and although Daniel wasn't scared, he remembered Damián's letters.

"Hey!"he shouted to the others inside. "We have visitors!'

As soon as Joacaría saw the fat man, he started to scream frantically, reverting to his Yiddish mother-tongue: "Kish me in tochis!"No more sophisticated French for now.

"Tell the bird to shut the fuck up!"said the shorter man. Standing there in the middle of the living room, the pair of pigs looked like a local version of Laurel and Hardy -even dressed like them. Nevertheless, they couldn't kid themselves. This was for real. These were secret police.

Joacaría understood the situation right away, and kept his beak shut for the rest of the time. There was a special twinkle in the bird's eyes: back from his fantasy trip to Montparnasse, Joacaría seemed amused rather than afraid.

"Papers!"demanded detective Oliver Hardy. The two women produced their identity cards; Luigi and Daniel did the same with their passports. After a cursory glance at them, the detective announced, "OK, we're going to take a look around."

"How about a cup of coffee?"asked Luigi. The two men looked a bit surprised; they shook their heads. "I'll prepare some for us, then."He disappeared into the kitchen while Laurel and Hardy moved along the corridor toward the bedrooms. Soon they could be heard opening and closing the doors of wardrobes, pulling out drawers, going through papers.

"Does anybody have any marihuana?"Wanda asked in a whisper. "I don't,"Olinda said. Daniel followed with, "As far as I know, Luigi and I don't either."*Maconha* in the house would have been bad enough, but these people were after something else: books, pamphlets, any kind of literature that would confirm their expectations of a communist conspiracy. The most prized find, of course, would have been a complete address book, with the names of lots of militants. A few weeks earlier, without any of them noticing, Olinda had removed anything that could have been used as evidence. A useless gesture: if they wanted to nail her, her paintings spoke loud and clear. Anyway, she had had a police file for years, they knew all about her.

"Who is this?"Stan Laurel shouted from one of the bedrooms. It was the poster of Ché Guevara. Daniel ran to the room:

"Who?"Then, looking at the poster, he said, "Ah, him ... it's Gilberto Gil."

"Who the hell is he?"Laurel asked. It was unmistakably el Ché, but it was a very dark, black and white photograph; the smoke from the cigar in his hand blurred some of his features.

"He's a singer, not very well-known, but the boy is promising,"said Daniel, aware that he shouldn't make the policeman feel patronised. "Should I play you some of his music? You must have heard of Caetano Veloso, Gilberto Gil is a friend of his."

Laurel seemed suspicious. "I'm sure I've seen his picture somewhere else."Daniel was quite convinced that, in a corner of his tiny, useless brain, the policeman had correctly identified the photograph. In any case, the two cops seemed to be going through the motions.

Back in the living room, Hardy asked Olinda: "Where is your son?'

"What's it to you?"Olinda burst out, indignant. A tactical mistake, she immediately realised. The pigs wanted to be provoked. Fatso grabbed her arm and forced her to sit on a chair. "You're not going to tell me what my business is, you, fucking Bolshevik. How many times have we brought you in already? Do you want to go back to jail? What are you all doing here, living together? We've been watching you, are you a cell? Or what?'

The only noise to be heard was Laurel's heavy breathing: he was wheezing, probably asthmatic. Daniel was silently pleading for Olinda not to lose her cool.

"He's up north with his grandparents, they live by the Sâo Francisco, he's going to school there,"Wanda intervened. She had many years of dealing with the police, and knew how to handle them. She added, "He's destined to be a great man."

"I don't give a shit where the boy is, *entendeu* - understand? I want you to tell me, clearly, who you are, each of you, and what the fuck you do. Age, address, employment. Clearly! Get it?'

It wasn't difficult: Olinda Morais, widow and painter. Luigi Marino, single and writer. Daniel Goldstein, single and poet. Wanda Ribeiro, single and inspiratrice.

Inspiratrice?

Fatso asked the questions while the other one wrote everything down. Neither of them dared to show their ignorance when Wanda stated her occupation.

"You don't look like *guerrilleros*, you probably couldn't kill a fly, but watch it, you'd better stay out of trouble. This was a routine inspection. We know everything there is to know about everyone, and there is a war out there."

Daniel had heard this before.

"Thanks for the advice,"Wanda said.

And that was it. For the time being, anyhow.

Once the cops left, Olinda led them out to the patio. "I need some fresh air,"she said.

She asked Luigi to take out a couple of blankets, which she spread side by side on the tiled floor. The four of them lay down, their heads together in the middle, looking at the sky: the evening star had appeared. They remained in silence for a long while, recovering, enjoying the sounds of the jungle. The cops' visit had shaken them. Now they were grateful; thankfully, nothing nasty had happened, and they were still together. Luigi produced a joint, which he had kept hidden inside one of his socks; this was duly celebrated by all. A small but sweet revenge. It was good to get high, to celebrate the existence of *inspiratrices*. They rocked with laughter remembering it.

"What's an *inspiratrice*?"Daniel demanded.

"A woman who inspires poets to write the best love poems," she said.

"Rio is crawling with gangsters, criminals and ruffians; instead, the sons of bitches are after an artist who is a member of the Communist Party, the most inoffensive party in the history of Latin America -they couldn't recognise a revolution even when Fidel was entering La Habana, and I'm not even an active member of the fucking Party anyhow ... Before my son was born, I didn't mind being taken to jail; it was a way of showing my solidarity with so many oppressed people across the globe -it was a privilege. I suppose I've been lucky, I was never tortured or mistreated; I was too well known for them to do anything to me. On the other hand, being famous has made me an easy target. If I were to disappear, what would happen to David? I'm pleased he's with my parents, but I miss him."

At that moment, Daniel wished David to be there, with them. For Olinda, for David, for himself. Although it was understandable that Olinda should have sent him away to his grandparents, there was something missing in the flat. His toys and his empty bed were daily reminders of his absence. Olinda became melancholic.

"My father was a *barqueiro*, he took the boat up and down the river, bringing flour, sugar, salt, and from time to time a bit of *maconha* as a present for the few policemen and officials in the distant towns. In the summer, he used to take me with him; he had woven a small hammock for me to sleep on the boat. At night, he'd lie in his, and I would be in mine, and he would teach me the names of the stars."

Sometimes, if her father fell asleep first, she lay awake for a long time; alone and alert to the nocturnal noises of the nearby jungle in the middle of those hot velvety nights, a sinister feeling would invade her. At those moments, she thought she could feel the presence of the *bicho da água*, the mythical monster that lived at the bottom of the river. People prayed to it and threw tobacco and medicinal herbs into the river to appease it. When it was angry, people said it came out of the waters and took young virgins away with him, hiding under the thick blanket of fog in the night. From her hammock, she could hear dogs on the riverbank, barking to announce the *bicho*'s presence. It terrified her.

"I saw small blobs of yellow light moving over the houses by the water, as it peeped through open windows to choose its victims. Phantom boats were occasionally reported carrying the bodies drowned, dressed in long black robes. People said that cattle that came to the river to drink were swallowed by the *bicho*."

Perhaps in response to Olinda, Wanda started to sing a tender lullaby, the same one that her grandmother had sung to her mother, who in turn had sung it to Wanda every night for many years. It had strange words and Yoruba names. Wanda told them that the lyrics spoke of a legendary continent, a mythical place where black people had originally come from, a land where hunger was unknown and freedom was possible.

They fell silent again until Daniel said, "I was picked up by the police a few times. Once, I was caught at a friend's house, a girl involved with the *guerrillas*. I was lucky, I was released after twenty-four hours. But it was shocking to see how many informers there were among people I knew. While I sat on a bench in the police headquarters in calle Moreno, waiting to be taken in for questioning, I saw dozens of people busily walking up and down the hall with papers and files – faces I had seen many times in the bar La Paz, in El Politeama, in the Cine Lorraine, in the bookshops of Avenida Corrientes: they were all a bunch of shit-faced snitches!"The thugs in charge knew how to create terror, how to spread fear and mistrust; they exercised an evil power, as much in Argentina as in the rest of the continent.

In fact, sooner or later the birds of evil omen were bound to arrive. To see them finally there, in that colonial house on the morro de Santa Teresa, had not come as a surprise. The repression was becoming more organised and efficient , no stone was left unturned. After the coup that got rid of Goulart, it was obvious. Olinda's turn would come too. A few weeks earlier, she had suggested that they all move somewhere else. She had sold many of her paintings to a Spanish aristocrat with whom she had become good friends. The Spanish woman owned a mansion in the Recreio dos Bandeirantes – a quiet beach at the end of the line of a number of bus routes. It was a safe place to stay, the countess had contacts in the army, the police would never dare to raid her house. But, at the time, none of them had taken Olinda's proposal too seriously.

Wanda finally asked out of the blue: "Why do you think that men can't say "I love you" to a woman?"

Unforgettable Wanda. Great timing. Olinda and Daniel giggled, while Luigi remained deadly serious. Daniel couldn't ignore it, he suggested she asked Luigi, "He knows about these things."

Luigi rose to the challenge, "Why is it so important? It's only words; women are so wrapped up in themselves; what counts is the feeling, not the words."

"As if you didn't like it when I say sweet things to you,"said Olinda.

"Of course I do,"admitted Luigi.

"So what stops you from saying them to Olinda?" asked Wanda.

"Nothing! I do tell her things,"he protested.

"What a liar!'

"I'm no liar; I say it with my eyes and my gestures, I shout it with my body and my actions."

"We're talking about words,"Daniel put in, just to be provocative; he knew that Wanda was right. "After all, a lot of us write love poems and songs and novels full of passion." He recited:

I love you with all the drummings of the rain...

"Maybe they just don't feel it,"Wanda ventured. That hurt, but wasn't true.

"Babies, that's what they are, those little things,"a cracked voice descending from the skies jolted them. It was the old woman who had watched Daniel having a shower on his first day at Olinda's. "You should see my old man suckling at my breasts, my poor boobs are tired and dried up, but he's still at it, sucking away as if they spouted *cachaça*. Y'know what they say, "Women's tits pull harder than a team of oxen." I tell you, they're all puppies, that's what they are; they want to suck, not speak. My old man never says nothin'..."

"*Nossa!* she's crazy,"Olinda whispered. And then, looking up, she said to the woman, "Good evening, Doña Teresinha, *tudo bem?*"

"*Tudo bom* − everything is OK. These warm nights are so beautiful, they fill me with an inconsolable love, but it's hard to be alone, this *saudade* is killing me."

She was aware, in spite of her madness, that she was all by

herself. No old man living with her, sucking her tits. All of them knew that Teresinha's husband had been dead for as long as Olinda could remember.

4

They thought that the omens had to do with the cops, but Wanda went on having nightmares. Then, she began to feel ill; occasionally, she felt like dying.

Meanwhile, Olinda became intensely absorbed in a new series of paintings. After Daniel's short and intense poetic absence, she was now living in a world of her own, disconnected from the rest of the group, apparently unconcerned about Wanda's suffering.

Wanda didn't want to talk much about it all. One day she brought a few herbs from the market, mixed them and boiled them to make an infusion. She took this aromatic brew every night before going to bed. Since she was so happy for most of the day, Wanda reassured Daniel that there was no reason to be worried. Daniel was persuaded to abandon his wish to take her to a doctor.

And then, to their relief, Wanda started feeling alright again.

Most nights, Wanda interrupted Daniel deepest sleep to tell him her nightmares. Much as they terrified her, she was upset by the fact that they didn't last long; the dreams were fleeting and precarious, she wanted them to stay longer in her mind.

"I feel somebody is writing them for me in water. It doesn't give me enough time to understand them. I would like to feel more committed to them."

Committed, a new word learnt from Olinda.

"It should be a relief that they don't last for ever,"Daniel offered as consolation.

"Yes, I'm also afraid of being caught in the dream, terrified that I won't be able to come back, and yet I want to be *there*. Do you think I'm going mad?'

"We are all pretty mad, it can't get any worse."Daniel embraced her, he stroked her hair and kissed her ears. He felt her relax in his arms. "There's nothing like cuddling for you, I love you for that."

"Sweet words, but in matters of love, you shouldn't lie."

"How can you call me a liar?'

"Easy."

"Obviously, there is no way to win: if I don't say anything, you complain; and if I say sweet nothings, I'm a liar."

"That's the way it is."

On those days, in spite of the worries, they made love as soon as they woke up; then went for walks, sometimes strolling around the hilly, twisted streets of old Rio, admiring the decaying colonial houses, the Carmelite Convent, the Hotel Santa Teresa, the Vista Alegre, the Largo de Guimaràes. They usually ended up at the Bar Waldemar, which opened at noon – the perfect time to have a cup of sweet coffee and smoke their first cigarette. Thankfully, Daniel's grant stretched a long way.

When she felt wretched, one of the few things that warmed Wanda's heart was George Brassens' music.

"Shall I tell you something?'

"What?'

"At the beginning, on the few occasions when I was by myself, that music made me come."He looked at her in disbelief, but Wanda didn't bullshit about those things. Under her dark skin, she had gone red.

"Just with the music?'

"He touched me with his voice in such a way that my whole body vibrated."

Daniel decided right then and there to grow a moustache, learn French, change his accent, and take singing lessons.

"It makes me jealous,"he admitted.

"It's only a voice."

"That makes it worse, I can't compete with him."

"Now, when I listen to him, it evokes a completely different feeling, I feel warm and safe and protected by him; he reminds me of my father. When I was three or four, I used to get into my parents' bed and play with the hair on his chest while lying in his arms. I loved him so …'

In spite of the cruel separation from the family that her father had imposed on her, Wanda always spoke of him with special fondness. Although sad, she never felt resentful. Looking at her, seeing the big tears run down her cheeks, Daniel realised how much he loved her.

Then one day Wanda started to feel ill again.

"My mother visited me in a dream last night, she was standing in the middle of a small sailboat, all by herself; she didn't seem to be in control of it. The boat was moving slowly, helped more by the current of the wide river than by its sail; she was opening and closing her mouth like a fish. She saw me standing on the riverbank and waved to me, then said, "Let's celebrate your excesses." Isn't that strange? What do you think she could have meant?"

"I don't know."

"I'm afraid of being punished for my happiness."

"That doesn't make sense,"said Daniel, knowing full well that he too had been thinking of the evil eye and horrible curses. "I think we should go to the doctor, enough of those teas that you make."He was afraid, what was wrong with Wanda?

Olinda, coming down from the creative clouds she had been inhabiting for a while, suggested they go see her *pai-de-santo* instead. He would be able to tell them whether it was a physical ailment or the result of a malevolent spell against Wanda.

"So much for your dialectical materialism! I just wonder what the Party would say about this,"Daniel taunted her.

"Everybody in Brazil goes to church as much as to the *terreiro*. In the case of my comrades, they might oppose religion officially, but they also respect *a macumba*. Just in case."

He was intrigued by the idea. "Don't get so agitated,"Wanda told him, "this is just a visit to the *pai-de-santo*, not a full ceremony."

"*Just a visit*"? It was not that simple. They had been warned many times about the danger in the *favelas*, where the *pai-de-santo* lived. And if they were assaulted? No foreigners would dare to go there; he had to trust Olinda's judgement. She was known by the people in the *favela*, and gave free drawing lessons to some of the kids. In fact, Olinda made the necessary arrangements through one of her pupils. It should be OK.

The entrance to the shanty town was innocent enough: a gate, leading to a narrow path that wound down the hill. Luigi and Daniel followed Olinda and Wanda, who were laughing and chatting at the top of their voices; the women were definitely not afraid, and seemed to jump from one subject to the next with equal passion.

"Have you ever been touched by a mystical call?"Luigi asked Daniel.

"Never! What about you?'

"No, never."

"One of my cousins became very interested in these mystical things; he told me about his experiences with great enthusiasm but I was never interested."

"Since when do you have a cousin? You never told me you had cousins."

"What's *that* got to do with anything? Of course I never told you I had cousins. So what? You don't know everything about me."

"I find it strange that you never told me that you had cousins."

"I have four first cousins and four second cousins. Happy now?'

"I don't care about the details, I just thought it was strange that you hadn't ever said you had cousins,"insisted Luigi.

A dialogue of the deaf. Daniel recognised Luigi's mood: he called it "transcendental stubbornness'. They were both anxious.

They walked slowly past the windows of the shacks, furtively glancing inside. By now, Olinda and Wanda had lowered their voices, saying very little. The hovels were crammed together. They were made of an assortment of bricks, breeze-blocks, cardboard boxes and bits of wood; a few of them had walls made of corrugated iron. The smell of plantain frying in *dendé* oil sweetened the air. Protected by the darkness, Daniel felt uncomfortable at looking through the bare windows. As in many other households around the world, the centre of family life was the TV, blazing at full volume, offering unattainable dreams to people of such extreme poverty.

They came to a small kiosk that sold *cachaça*, rice, black beans and sugar. The sparse supplies were on display on a counter made from an old door laid over two pairs of empty wooden fruit crates. The shop owner behind the improvised counter was talking to two other men. Holding beer bottles in their hands, they smiled at the newcomers, showing their rotten teeth; all of them looked older than they were.

"Good evening,"Olinda greeted them. "Is Dom Severino at home?'

"I guess so, I didn't see him leaving today, go ahead, you know where it is, don't you?"Olinda thanked him and signalled to the others to follow her.

Narrow alleys branched off from the main path, winding up and down the hill; they were the only means of access to hundreds of huts hidden behind the ones at the front. Olinda stopped at the entrance to one of them; she seemed to be trying to recognise the place in the darkness. They were all standing in silence, watching her, when rain started to bucket down. They let the rain wet their faces as they looked up at a black velvety sky, full of stars, at a loss to explain where the rain was coming from.

Daniel unexpectedly remembered the poem he had thought of while returning from the police station with Wanda, "Memory held us wild and loving..." Now, he could suddenly place its source. It was a distortion of Dylan Thomas's poem, "Time held me green and dying, though I sang in my chains like the sea ..."

"Where are you?"Luigi asked.

"I'm here,"Daniel answered, wondering how come it was raining on that little patch, just above that house. Everywhere else seemed to be dry.

"This place is a bit spooky, it even smells different."

He agreed. The rain had a strange blend of aromas, with a penetrating scent of citrus.

Olinda walked straight into the shack unannounced. Everybody else followed. Inside, there wasn't much furniture, just a chair and a small table in a corner. An archway with a bead curtain opened on to another room. Squatting on the floor, which was entirely covered by straw mats, was Dom Severino. While the rest of the huts in the *favela* had electricity stolen from the streetlights of Santa Teresa, this one was lit by candles; they created a warm and welcoming atmosphere.

"I received your message, I was waiting for you. Who is the afflicted one?"Dom Severino asked. He stood up, all dressed in white, a pair of cotton trousers and an unbuttoned shirt. He had slightly sunken cheeks, and this became more noticeable when he sucked on a cigar held between his teeth. His hair was long and grey, with curls springing up like a worn-out toupee.

Wanda stepped forward. Daniel felt the impulse to hold her hand and accompany her but, instead, he followed Olinda's lead and sat with her and Luigi on the floor, in a corner. In the middle of the most profound silence, Luigi leaned over and whispered in his ear:

"Have I told you that my father was one-eyed?'

He tried to find Luigi's face in the penumbra, making a supreme effort not to burst out laughing.

"Why do you tell me this now?"

"You told me about your cousins, so now I'm telling you about my father."

Olinda begged them to shut up; Dom Severino was ready to start the ceremony. Daniel thought: *"Tano bruto! -dumb Italian!'*

Dom Severino asked Wanda to take off her shoes and sit on the floor right in front of him. A circle of light illuminated the space between the *pai-de-santo* and Wanda. The old man gave her a piece of paper and a pen, and asked her to write down her name and date of birth. He brought out some cowrie shells, all of similar size; their bases had been cut so they could stand on end. He placed them on the floor beside them. He started to recite different prayers: first, to Oxalá, the God of all Gods, the Creator. The *pai* explained to Wanda that they weren't going to ask him for anything: "He is the best of all our divinities, but he's busy with very important things and sometimes he's tired, we won't bother him. We'll just invoke his blessing."

This was followed by more prayers: to the dead first of all, and then to the numerous *orixás* – the gods of the Yorubas. Olinda had explained that everyone was supposed to have his or her own *orixá*, who looked after the person's spirit and protected it from evil. The *pai-de-santo* identified individually which *orixá* was assigned to a person. Dom Severino took the shells in his hands and offered further prayers in Yoruba; then he blew on them. Afterwards, he said to Wanda:

"You have to do the same; this will give them *axé*. Only then will they help us."

Wanda followed the instructions and blew onto the *búzios* to awaken their powers. Any temptation to laugh had long passed; Olinda, Luigi and Daniel followed the proceedings closely. The *pai* threw the shells on the mat. There were sixteen pieces; eleven of them landed on the ground with their natural openings facing upwards.

"Drawing water with a basket..."murmured Dom Severino, and then he fell into a deep silence.

Daniel could feel, without even looking at her, that Olinda's expression had changed: a shadow had covered her face. Finally, the *pai* spoke to Wanda again:

"Did you know that your father died?'

He asked the question in such a matter of fact way that they almost missed it.

"Don't worry, child,"the *pai* continued. "He quickly realised that he had chosen the wrong time to do so, that he shouldn't have gone without sorting things out with you, so he woke up soon after and decided to come back to life again. He's waiting for you, sitting outside in a patio, under a tree. In fact, it's a Tree of Heaven. You have to find a way of resolving the differences with your people: your father has forgiven you, and I know there is no revenge in your heart, you can be sure that Oiá and Exú are protecting you."

Exú! He remembered that Exú was the god that had chosen Eugenio, their murdered friend, to spread the divine message. Luigi too had registered the name.

"Oiá, the goddess of storms and strong winds and the owner of all burial places, stands at the door of cemeteries. As one of the wives of Xangó, the only god with power over the dead, she denied your father the right to enter his grave and forced him to wake up. You should be especially grateful to her."

Dom Severino spoke slowly and clearly.

"You should remember: she likes aubergines, goats and hens, she'll welcome your offerings."

It sounded like a request for presents; the gods were quite greedy. Why not? Food was better than money.

"As far as Exú is concerned, he's a trickster by nature and he's been quite mischievous, playing with his powers. He's generous and compassionate, but has tricked you in some way, I couldn't say how. We can't tell when Exú is fair or not, but he can change anybody's destiny. There is one thing: a death is following you." The silence in the room deepened. Dom Severino continued, "you have to be on good terms with Exú: he loves to eat just about everything – and he eats a lot! Lamb and chicken; pigeon, sparrow and yellowhammer; suckling pig and multicoloured hen; guava and custard apple. And if you really want to gain his favour, offer him plenty of *cachaça* and *caruru*. That makes him very happy, he starts dancing and fooling around, and that is when he grants everything you ask him for. Perhaps you should also offer him a mass at the Church."

Daniel and Luigi had tried *caruru*; it was the dish that Fulvio had cooked for them on that memorable first night with the transvestites. Exú was no fool, he knew how to choose his food. The wise old man had guessed correctly at Wanda's and her father's quarrel, but were Dom Severino's perceptions authentic?

When they returned, Joacaría greeted them with friendly chirps.

"Do you see that? He's smiling!"

Daniel also thought the bird was flashing a smile when they came in. He was in a good mood and moved from one person to another, chattering away, bobbing his head up and down, happy to see them. "What's the good news, *amigo?*" Daniel asked the parrot.

Olinda and Luigi sat together on the sofa, Daniel on the floor leaning against the bookcase; Wanda stretched on the carpet, her head resting on his lap. She was withdrawn and sad. Daniel stroked her head.

"The *pai* said that a death was following you,"Olinda said, looking at Wanda. "Do you have any idea what he meant? Is there anybody else in your family beside your father who's old or might be ill?"Wanda shook her head, she didn't think so, she didn't know.

"Maybe it was your father after all,"suggested Luigi, "but fortunately he's come back, so there's nothing to worry about."He was trying his best to sound optimistic, but wasn't that convincing. Dom Severino had been clear; he was referring to yet another death, a tragedy to come.

After all that ceremony, they were still in the dark. What was really wrong with Wanda? He couldn't deny it: Daniel hated the thought of her being ill. He had refused to consider her nightmares as real omens, as signs or portents of future deaths. He didn't easily believe in that sort of thing; he was worried, and was determined to take her to a doctor.

In one of her nightmares, Wanda had seen candles floating just above the fields surrounding her house. She herself was floating above the ground, unable – despite her efforts – to reach down with her feet. She was in a panic because the flames were blue, which meant, Wanda thought, that the death foretold was that of a child. If only she could touch the ground, the child would be saved. She wriggled and bent and stretched down, but remained suspended in the air.

In another dream, she saw her mother in the middle of a row of beehives. In fact, Wanda's father kept bees in a field near their home. Her mother was delicately tapping three times with a wooden spoon on the roof of each hive while telling the bees that her husband had gone on a long trip. Wanda saw her mother wearing a black ribbon on her head. Her parents' house, far on the horizon, was covered by loose black sheets that floated in the wind.

And there was another nightmare that had left Wanda feeling upset and confused: a boy lay asleep on a wooden bed without a mattress. He was still and looked calm. The peacefulness of the scene was broken by somebody who yanked the pillow out from under the boy's head. Daniel couldn't forget that dream, Wanda had felt she could hear the thump of the boy's head hitting the hard surface beneath him.

"I might be pregnant."

Wanda's words were hardly audible in the middle of the deafening noise produced by the tree frogs from the jungle. It took a few seconds for her announcement to get through to everybody.

"I didn't want to think about it, I might have missed a period, it's just a possibility, I feel so bad."

Olinda was the first to react; she smiled and said to Wanda: "*Meu Deus, mulher!* -My God, woman! How stupid of me, where has my head been? Why didn't I think of it before?"She stood up and held Wanda's head between her hands and kissed her on both cheeks. "*Nossa Senhora do Bonfim!* It's not death then, it's life we're celebrating."

Olinda turned to Luigi and offered him her hand: "Come on."Luigi looked at her, glanced at Wanda and Daniel: "Yeah, let's go."They both said goodnight and disappeared into their bedroom. Just like that. Incredible.

"Great!"thought Daniel. "What a time to be randy!"Lust followed strange paths. He was slow to react, still thinking about Wanda's dreams. And now, what? He felt lost. A few minutes ago, Wanda was ill; now, she might be pregnant –quite a difference! Was he the father of a child?

The room felt empty, as if it had suddenly grown enormous. The night was cool; now, there was very little noise coming through the window -the frogs had suddenly stopped their racket. Wanda covered herself with the blanket Olinda had draped over the tattered and dirty sofa.

"How did it happen?"

"What?'

"That you got pregnant."

"Shall I tell you the story of the little seed?"

"You know what I mean,"Daniel felt like a fool. "I mean, are you sure?'

"About what?'

"Being pregnant."

"No, of course I'm not sure. I'll have a test tomorrow."

"This is very strange. How come nobody thought of it before? It's so obvious!"

"You told me once that the obvious is the most difficult thing to see."

"And if you were pregnant?'

Wanda raised her head to look at him. She was smiling but her eyes were sad. "It'll mean you're the father."

"I wonder what my own father would say", Daniel thought. What other stupidities would he think next?

"You should feel proud you're fertile."Wanda's generosity put him to shame.

"I do feel proud, but…'

"What?'

"I'm not sure."

"Don't be silly,"Wanda exclaimed. "I knew I was fertile, remember? It was your turn."

"You're making me feel good for something I've done to you."

"What do you think you've done to me?"

"I've made you pregnant."

"Why is that so bad?'

He couldn't explain.

When the call from the doctor's surgery finally came through, Daniel was alone in the house having a shower. The telephone rang for a long time. He stumbled out of the bathroom still wet, shampoo running down his face.

"Hello?"he shouted.

"Could I speak to Miss Ribeiro please?"The female voice sounded formal and efficient. He was so surprised to hear Wanda's surname that he almost said "wrong number'.

"Who's this?"He didn't feel being polite.

"This is Dr Da Costa's surgery. Could you ask Miss Ribeiro to give us a ring? We have the results of the pregnancy test."

The nurse immediately realised that she had made a mistake. She shouldn't have mentioned the test.

"This is Daniel, her husband, could you give me the results, please?'

Now he'd really put his foot in it! If he was trying to convince her, it wasn't a clever tactic. After a pause, he heard her saying: "I didn't know *Miss* Ribeiro was married."

"No, I'm sorry,"he apologised. "I'm Wanda's boyfriend, I just wanted to know. I hope you understand. These are difficult times for us."

Pathetic, trying now to make her feel sorry. She didn't respond. She had gone back to her role as competent nurse. He could almost hear her thinking, weighing the circumstances.

"That wasn't very successful, was it?"

There she was once again, the voice descending from the sky – except that this time Doña Teresinha was sitting right behind him, in the middle of the sofa. She wore a crumpled white organdie dress which had gone yellow; it had probably been made a long time ago for a Carnival procession by a samba school. Her skinny old body could be seen through the thin material. She was holding a dish covered with brown paper on her lap. How come he hadn't seen her coming in? How did she get in, anyway? And why was she all dressed up in that absurd outfit?

"What are you doing here?'

"What do you mean?"said the nurse on the phone. "No, no, I'm sorry, I wasn't talking to you."He tried to change the tone. "Could you ask Dr Da Costa whether he would agree to give me the results over the phone? It's important." "I'll see what I can do."No sympathy whatsoever.

Why was it his destiny to be exposed naked to this crazy old lady? Daniel looked around for something to cover himself with. He picked up the dishcloth that had been left on the chair next to the phone. It had a print of the statue of Cristo Redentor on top of the Corcovado. It said in big letters: *Cidade Maravilhosa*. He held it with one hand on his belly and let it drop down to cover his genitals.

"I've seen this movie before", he thought to himself.

"You have a very nice bum,"Doña Teresinha said. "It's round and sweet and inviting, not all men have handsome asses."

What to say? Doña Teresinha was quite a character. Although he had a certain romantic sympathy for mad people, he was a bit intimidated by them. It was one thing to read André Breton and fall in love with Nadja at a distance. It was quite another to be alone and naked in a room with an old lady, dressed as a girl, lost on her way to her first communion. It was unlikely, but what if she had a knife hidden under the brown paper?

"My old man has a big ass, not very attractive,"Doña Teresinha continued. Daniel was still waiting for the nurse to come back. "But I love him anyway; he has given me a very happy life."

Poor Doña Teresinha.

"You don't believe me, do you?"She said it with such a look that – just for a split second – Daniel thought she might have been putting him on. Maybe she wasn't mad after all.

"Yes, of course I believe you."He wasn't lying.

"I brought Olinda some cakes, they're her favourites, my old man used to like them very much."

Now she spoke in the past! She was acknowledging her husband's death.

"His favourite dish though is fried snakes."

Here we go again.

"You shouldn't be surprised, snake meat is really delicious: white and clean like the flesh of a virgin."She was getting poetic.

"Where is the bloody nurse?" he thought.

"It doesn't matter whether they're poisonous or not, you should always hack their heads off for cooking. He likes watching me skinning them and cutting up the meat. The best way to cook them is to marinate them first in orange and lemon juice with pepper and nutmeg. Then, after a few hours, I dip them in egg and breadcrumbs and fry them in butter. He goes wild!'

Wild, indeed. Next to the old woman, how could he not have become irredeemably mad?

It was taking ages for the nurse to come back to the phone. For the first time, Daniel noticed Joacaría in a corner of the room, hiding behind the little palm trees that Olinda kept in colourful painted pots; the parrot looked suspicious and wary. It occurred to Daniel that the subject of conversation might be the cause of the bird's mood. Daniel had recently seen *papagaio recheado* advertised in the window of a restaurant. "Don't worry," he said to Joacaría in his mind, "you're too old to be stuffed and eaten, you must be tougher than a wet rope sandal."

"Nobody says much about it, but women find men's asses very attractive."Doña Teresinha didn't give up that easily. "The skin is where it all begins, not the colour or the texture, but its smell: there are aromas of bread, seaweed, lavender, fire, monkey, or moonshine ... After the skin, it's the eyes, "the windows to the soul", as my mother used to say. Then, the shape of the ass, you should definitely be aware of it: your ass is inspiring."

"Look, Doña Teresinha, I do appreciate your interest, but a lot of things are happening right now, you know? Life is kind of complicated, I'm getting cold and... I'm not very keen to discuss my ass!'

"I beg your pardon?"said Dr Da Costa on the line.

"I'm sorry, Doctor, I was talking to my neighbour,"Daniel apologised just as quickly, realising that the less he explained the better. "My name is Daniel Goldstein, I'm Miss Ribeiro's boyfriend; I know about the pregnancy test, in fact I am ... well, I mean ... I might be the father of the child."

"Which child?"the doctor asked.

"Oh, so she's not pregnant."

"I didn't say so."

"Well, either she is or she is not pregnant, one or the other."

"I don't see any reason for me to tell you anything about one of my patients."

"Except that I happen to be your patient's boyfriend, I might have some curiosity to know whether she's pregnant or not."

"I understand you lied to my nurse, pretending to be Miss Ribeiro's husband."

"True."The shampoo was stinging his eyes. "I'll tell Wanda to call you as soon as she comes in,"he said in a dignified tone. And before hanging up he added, "I'm sorry."

In the meantime, Doña Teresinha had fetched a couple of big towels from the cupboard. She shook them open and put them on Daniel"shoulders. He felt small and broken. As he walked down the corridor, he turned around to say something to her but she was no longer there. He retraced his steps and ran to the front door. It was still locked from inside.

5

Who said that youth was a happy time?
Even when Daniel felt on top of the world, when he was with Wanda and it seemed nothing could threaten his happiness, or when he'd written a good poem, even then, in those rare moments, there was an anguish, an *angst* -a word that Luigi had taught him, which they translated as "existential pungency". It permeated everything he did. He didn't think that the world and life were meaningless -that feeling had long gone. Nor did he have ideas of suicide or violent fantasies of impossible revolutions. It was more like a persistent, relentless *saudade*: a painful mixture of nostalgia, sorrow and homesickness -a longing that could never be fulfilled.

Saudade -another word impossible to translate.

Nevertheless, on that unforgettable day Daniel woke up with a more specific pain: he had had a dream in which someone, who seemed to have been hanging like a heavy coat among the rest of the clothes in their wardrobe, suddenly fell to the ground. It could have been one of Wanda's nightmares. He woke up with a shout, thinking, *somebody has died*. Daniel felt a great ache in his chest, and for just an instant thought that he was having a heart attack. Of course he wasn't. He stayed in bed for a while, thinking about the abortion, which was due to take place later that day. Had this inspired the dream? He also remembered Damián; he thought about his last letter. As children, they met after school to play soccer with the other kids from the local gang, on calle Gurruchaga. Damián was talented; he played with humour, always enjoyed himself, and never got into a fight. Everyone admired him. Older than most of the other boys, he became a real star when he was the first to ejaculate. A group of them sat around in a semicircle on a rainy autumn day, just outside the open door of the lift in the building where Damián lived. He demonstrated the production of a viscous, slightly off white, creamy liquid. Wow! Amazing. It spurted onto the tiled floor and remained there for the caretaker to clean up.

Damián and Daniel had taken different paths. His friend became a taxi driver, which allowed him to earn a living while devoting himself to being *un rockero*, a rock'n'roll singer. It didn't last long. Damián went back to studying and qualified as a teacher. He also got married, had a couple of kids, and worked hard to keep his family; he taught at a private school during the day, and tutored students at home in the evenings. His real ambition was to become a writer. What was going to happen to him now? Things must have been truly bad in Argentina, his friend did not easily get depressed. Although he was a member of the Communist Party, Damián hadn't really ever been involved in politics. Daniel could not have imagined him being in any danger. Now his letters were telling another story.

After the initial shock, Wanda accepted her pregnancy as a natural event. She had calmly made the decision to have an abortion; there hadn't been any discussion about it. Daniel felt hurt that she hadn't consulted him; it was out of his control. In fact, he didn't want a child, he didn't feel ready for a baby, and yet, he didn't like feeling ignored. He felt excluded from

Wanda and her body. As much as he might have wanted to possess her while making love, this was a fruitless desire. Neither Wanda nor the baby belonged to him. He felt expelled from Paradise.

That morning, Wanda had woken up early and prepared *um piquenique*. She had suggested the previous night that they go for an early lunch to Tijuca National Park.

"I'll prepare a picnic just for the two of us,"she said, "then you'll take me to the doctor. It's not far from Tijuca, it's in Leblon; he's a reputable doctor, you know."

Leblon, next to Ipanema, was a posh suburb in the southern part of Rio. Daniel doubted that it was going to be that close to the forest, Wanda wasn't famous for her sense of direction. At least the abortion was going to be performed by a professional – even if he was making his living from illegal operations. Daniel was certain that this was going to be expensive.

Wanda insisted on calling a taxi. "I'd like to be relaxed today, I don't want to get tired, I'll pay for it."

He was grateful that money had never been an issue among the four of them. Each had been generous with the little they had. Daniel couldn't have paid for the abortion, he didn't have the money – and Wanda wouldn't have accepted even a modest contribution.

She put everything in a basket and covered it with a bright blue tea cloth. "We shouldn't forget the wine, I bought the best I could find."

They had a shower together, which always made her happy. Afterwards, while she prepared a small leather bag with a change of clothes, he took the bottle of wine from the fridge and put it in the basket. Wanda had bought an Italian wine, a dry white called Frascati. It was the first time in his life that he would taste European wine. He felt puzzled: it was an abortion, and yet she was turning it into a celebration.

The Tijuca Forest was more beautiful than he could have imagined: a tropical jungle that had survived the explosive growth of the city; it had magnificent trees, clear streams and innumerable waterfalls. Wanda directed the taxi driver to take them to the entrance to the Alto da Boa Vista, where they were able to choose a perfect spot for their picnic.

"We're lucky,"Wanda told him, "on weekends this gets very crowded. Did you see the offerings by the roadside?"

Daniel had seen them: bottles of *cachaça*, piles of cigars, bunches of flowers of all colours, wooden dishes full of white corn, lots of little mirrors, candles, necklaces, pots of honey.

"What are they?'

"Candomblé,"she said without further explanation.

Candomblé, Macumba, Babassuê, Xangó, Batuque, Tambor, Pará – different names for the same African religion.

They chose a place near a waterfall. They spread a small blanket on the ground, still humid with the morning dew, and unpacked the food from the basket. There was no one around. The idyllic setting was spoiled only by the mosquitoes, which seemed to have a special inclination for Argentinian blood.

Wanda had prepared a feast. Daniel carefully set out the cold meats on a decorated paper plate while Wanda prepared a fresh *molho de pimenta*, a sauce of hot green chillies, crushed and mixed with lime juice in an improvised mortar of cup and spoon. Daniel opened the bottle of wine. He offered some to Wanda, but she refused.

"I shouldn't drink or eat anything, maybe I'll be given anaesthesia, my stomach should be empty. It's all for you."

Daniel felt rather self-conscious, all that food and wine just for him. Wanda urged him: "I want you to really enjoy this."

"I've never seen shrimps this big."

"The man at the shop where I bought them told me that these are caught when the moon is full, the time for lovers."

Wanda, incorrigibly romantic, thinking of full moons.

"Are you scared?'

"No, it's only going to be a d&c."And then, "Do you sometimes hear music in your head?'

"No, not really."

"I do, quite often. Sometimes I hear a piano playing a heavenly piece, I don't know where I heard it before, I must have picked it up from TV. But of course, most of the time now I hear Brassens."

"Oh, that bastard!'

"Sing me a tango! You said you couldn't compete with the Frenchman; well, here's your chance!'

He drank some more wine, got up, looked around to make sure there was nobody there, grabbed an imaginary microphone, and began to sing:

> *Percanta que me amuraste*
> *en lo mejor de mi vida,*
> *dejándome el alma herida*
> *y espinas en el corazón ...*

First, Wanda laughed and giggled, but then she looked at him admiringly, as if he were a real singer.

"That is *Mi Noche Triste* –My Sad Night, one of the most popular tangos in Argentina: a perfect example of kitsch, the pinnacle of creative pretentious nonsense, of pathetic self-pity."

Wanda interrupted him, "What is kitsch?'

"Just bad taste, I guess."

"But you sang it with passion and love."

"I was pretending."

"Bull! I know you weren't."

Wanda was right: in spite of his contempt for some of the lyrics, he was still moved by tango. He couldn't avoid it: "This tango made Carlos Gardel famous. I can even remember the date when he sang it for the first time: 1917, at the Teatro Esmeralda – later called Teatro Maipo."

"You know a lot about Gardel."

"Gardel died on 24 June, in a plane crash in Medellín. Some said that Carlitos had survived the crash and that he was living in the Colombian jungle; he didn't want to be seen, his face had been badly burnt and he was very vain. Once a year, on the anniversary of his death, I would watch three Gardel movies in a row at the Coliseo Palermo, a cinema close to my house."

"Were they good, those movies?'

"Atrocious! Absolutely unbelievable! I remember the date of his death, but for the life of me I can never remember either of my parents' birthdays, or Independence Day."

Wanda asked him to sit beside her; she refilled his glass of wine.

Those black eyes, he couldn't resist them. Maybe Doña Teresinha wasn't right after all: the eyes were more important than the skin. The day they met, it was Wanda's eyes that he had seen first.

"Do you know something?"

"What?"

"You make me grow up."

It was the strangest of compliments, the most loving thing any woman had ever said to him.

"You make me grow up too, Wanda – a lot!'

"At the beginning I couldn't believe you wanted me, a black whore from the streets of Lapa."

"Don't talk like that, I couldn't believe that you wanted me: a lost, young poet who couldn't offer you much."

"You all gave me your friendship. Nobody had done that before. You and Olinda and Luigi have changed my life."Tears welled up her eyes but she held them back. Then she changed her tone and said, "Enough of this soap opera! Guess what I've got here!'

She pulled out a condom, opened the package and blew it up. She got up and started hitting the balloon, trying not to let it fall on the ground. Daniel joined in the game, remembering the night they had met. Ironic, to play with a condom, given the circumstances.

"If you let it drop, you're a fool."

They ran around laughing and yelling until the balloon fell on a thorny bush and burst. It drooped at the end of a branch, blending in with the yellow flowers. Wanda took Daniel's hand and ran towards the trees. She stopped in a small clearing and turned around to kiss him; they embraced and dropped to the ground. It was cool and wet, the trees around them too dense for the midday sun to filter through. She obviously wanted him to take charge. They were tender and passionate. Daniel, aware of the imminent visit to the doctor, withdrew just in time. They remained on the ground, intertwined, hidden from the rest of the world.

"I really wanted this to be a party,"she whispered in his ear, "to make up for how awful my first abortion was. I don't feel like that now, I feel loved and free. It's a celebration of life, not death."

They walked back to the entrance to the Alto da Boa Vista and caught a bus to the Jardim Botânico. As they travelled down the mountain they felt the change of temperature; a tangible heat enveloped them. Then, they took a taxi that took them directly to Leblon.

Wanda knew of a small but friendly hotel, they could have a drink at the bar. Daniel waited for her there while she went to the toilet to wash and change into clean clothes. He asked for a *Brahma chopp* and sat at the counter. He wrote on a paper serviette:

> *I choose my place in the storm,*
> *an offering to her challenges,*
> *winds from the high sea,*
> *her body, open to heroism…*

Daniel quickly ordered another beer.

She has the right to sing the blues,
from the beginning
to say something unsuitable to the circumstances...

"What are you writing?"she asked, embracing him from behind, pressing against his back. Was it true about women's interest in men's asses?

"A shopping list,"he lied, promptly folding the paper and putting it in the pocket of his jeans. "Shall we go?'

"We should go."

He called the waiter, who didn't come; Daniel finished the beer, left the money on the counter and followed Wanda. She was already at the main entrance to the hotel, waiting for him and holding the door open. She was radiant, as she usually was after they made love.

"You look wonderful – are you wearing new clothes?"

"You noticed, I'm glad."

She was wearing a white embroidered blouse, buttoned down the front, and a pair of elegant green slacks. No bra. She had tied her hair with a silk scarf, with an abstract design.

"Are you going to write a poem for me one day?'

"No, never, it wouldn't do you justice, but one day I'll make a film about you, I'll call it *Garota de Lapa*."

"Doesn't sound good, what about *Menina de Manaus*? "

"It's a deal."Then, he asked her, "If one wants to say "girl", what's the difference between *garota* and *menina*?'

She shrugged her shoulders. Perhaps there was no difference.

"Remember what the *pai* told me?"Wanda asked.

"Which of the things he told you?'

"About my father, that he's waiting for me outside our house."

"Yes."Of course Daniel remembered; he had been anticipating this one.

"I'd like to see my father soon, otherwise he might not be able to die."And as an afterthought she added, "It's unfair to him, he might be tired of living. How long does he have to wait for me?'

Daniel nodded in agreement.

"I want you to come with me. You'll meet Pirata, the one-eyed cock that my mother spoiled rotten."

"I'm sure I'll enjoy meeting Pirata."

"We can also invite Olinda and Luigi,"said Wanda.

"Sure."

"And Joacaría."

"Yes, of course."

They arrived at the building they were looking for, typically smart and stylish: white marble at the entrance and big mirrors everywhere. An indoor garden and a little pond with a small waterfall gave it an air of unreality. The Portuguese *porteiro* at the door, a duster in his hand, pretended to be busy while looking them up and down. They said, "good morning'.

People living in those apartment buildings couldn't survive without the *porteiros*. In the morning they cleaned, polished the floors, and watered the gardens; everyone depended on them to repair leaky taps or a faulty washing machine. After the afternoon siesta they changed status, some might even dress up in a concierge's uniform. They looked like Prussian officers in charge of the ceremonial troops, jackets ablaze with silver buttons, standing at the main entrance like guard dogs. Nevertheless, their main task was to gather interesting gossip: they not only knew what was happening in their own building, but just about everything there was to know about everyone in the neighbourhood.

They got in the lift and went up to the fifth floor. Doctors weren't supposed to have their practices in residential buildings, but their neighbours usually turned a blind eye. There was a certain prestige in having a doctor in the house – even an abortionist.

The polished wooden door of the lift opened directly into the reception room. White dominated the décor: the walls, the lush heavy carpet, the desk, the bookshelves and the leather armchairs. "A world without children", thought Daniel.

Wanda walked straight to the receptionist, also in white, sitting behind the desk. She identified herself, and the woman stretched her mouth into a smile, as false as could be.

"The doctor is expecting you,"she said.

She ignored Daniel. She got up and directed Wanda to a pair of frosted glass doors. There was another hall behind the doors, with access to a number of rooms. The place looked like a clinic rather than the consulting room of a single doctor; the abortionist was a big shot, his illicit business was clearly profitable.

Wanda asked him to wish her good luck and disappeared through the doors. Daniel sat in one of the armchairs and picked up a couple of magazines from the huge coffee table in front of him – publications full of good-looking, happy people, luxurious houses, fast bright cars and exuberant gardens. Daniel read both magazines, feeling strange and out of place. He must have fallen asleep for a while because he woke suddenly with the sound of a door opening. Wanda reappeared. How much time had passed? He didn't have a clue. Minutes? A couple of hours? He was astonished to see her looking the same as before, elegant, composed. However, her face looked serious, the smile had gone from her lips, and her eyes were red.

Wanda walked decisively to the desk. She took a small bundle from her handbag; it was money wrapped in a handkerchief. It wasn't *just* money, it was American dollars! Daniel had never seen so many together. She counted some out under the attentive gaze of the woman, who put them away discreetly, without checking, in a metal box inside a drawer. The perfect black market deal: illegal operations performed by a reputable surgeon who got paid in foreign currency. Daniel felt tempted to ask for a signed receipt.

As they were leaving, Daniel discovered a crucifix carved in black wood right behind the receptionist's desk. Next to it, there was a small painting in blue ink of the *sertão* – one of the early works of Olinda Morais. The delinquent bourgeoisie consuming revolutionary art. As he opened the door of the lift, Daniel turned around and said to the receptionist:

"You should watch out, the police might want to pay you a visit. Did you know that you have a communist painting hanging on the wall?'

The receptionist had been efficient after all: a taxi was waiting for them at the door. At first, Daniel was too absorbed with Wanda – looking after her, making sure she was feeling comfortable – to notice who the driver was. But once the man started talking, his accent was unmistakable: of all the taxi drivers in a city of millions of people, they had to get the same Syrian lunatic who had been saving electricity by driving without lights at night. "What do you prefer for your Christmas dinner? Turkey or goose? In my family we traditionally ate goose; but recently, in the latest festivities, we had turkey. Which one would you say is better?'

He was unstoppable and Wanda seemed keen to take him on. "We never had goose at home,"she explained to Abdullah. "My mother would buy the live turkey at the market and bring it home to be fattened; by the time it was ready, it was as big as a calf."

"Really?"The driver became excited with the idea of a young cow with feathers. He was running red lights, crossing traffic lanes and turning his head to look at them. While Daniel grew more anxious, Wanda appeared compelled to continue talking to the madman. Maybe that distracted her, made her forget Dr Da Costa and his beastly receptionist.

"When the bird was ready to be killed, my father would take over,"Wanda continued. Daniel was trying to imagine Anselmo, her father, with a butcher's knife in his hand; he had become curious to meet him. "He would gather the rest of the family, friends and neighbours, and made the poor turkey drink a whole bottle of *cachaça*."

"Really? Didn't the bird die with so much alcohol in his body?"Daniel asked ingenuously.

"That was exactly the point!"said the Wise Man from Aleppo. Abdullah was too Muslim a name for him; if he were a Christian, Omar would fit him better.

"The turkey got completely pissed out of his mind,"Wanda asserted. "It died of happiness, a very pleasant death; what's more, you'll never taste meat as tender."

They arrived at Santa Teresa much quicker than expected. As he pulled up at the curb, Omar asked: "What do you do for a living?"The same question he had asked Luigi and Daniel that first time. Evidently, he hadn't recognised him.

"I'm a whore and he's a poet."

"A whore! And a poet! What a romantic combination!"Omar shouted through the window as he handed Daniel the change. Then, as he drove off, he called out knowingly, "I wish you both many years of happiness together! Your first son will be President of the Republic!'

Wanda took Daniel by the hand and squeezed it, guessing how Daniel might feel.

"Why didn't you ask him to recite you some poems in Arabic as well? He's quite good at it; I've met him before, with Luigi."

"Don't be so silly, *meu cachorrinho* – my puppy, there was no reason for him to know what's happening to us, or where we've come from."

It was the last straw. Daniel surprised himself; he stood crying in the middle of the pavement, unable to control himself. "Your first son will be President…"Motherfucker son of a bitch. He felt exposed, vulnerable, a child in a world he couldn't quite understand. At the same time, he was furious with himself for feeling that way. He wanted to be a real man, able to protect a woman and make her feel good, to love her and look after her. He regretted the abortion, to have exposed her to that pain. The combination of whore and poet was quite a romantic one, but how long could it last? Daniel had always imagined that one day he would end up living with a woman in a small house by the sea, away from it all, writing and walking his dog on the beach. Maybe it was better for Wanda to marry a madman like the taxi driver from Aleppo.

Wanda pressed her body against his, Daniel began to feel better. Slowly, they started to walk towards the house, still holding hands, in silence. As they entered it, Joacaría greeted them by performing a dance. It was a delight to watch him jumping about on his wooden leg, dancing to a samba that only he could hear. Olinda and Luigi were waiting for them in the kitchen, and welcomed them home. While waiting, they had moved the dining table outside and set it with flowers and candles. The old Chanukah lamp stood at one end, casting its soft light.

They all lingered after dinner in the back patio, enjoying the warmth of the night. Although it was hot during the day, it became pleasant and sensual once the sun was gone. To go to bed seemed a waste of time. Luigi had learned to roll long thin joints that offered an enjoyable, cool smoke. The candlelight made their arms and faces look dark bronze. Wanda didn't want to smoke; Daniel, though tempted, also refused the offer.

Olinda collected the dishes and took them to the kitchen. Usually, they all shared the domestic tasks; this time they let her look after them.

"Was it OK?"Luigi inquired after a while.

"Everything was fine."Then, a prolonged silence. Better that way.

"I've got something to tell you, Olinda got some grim news today,"Luigi announced.

"What?'

"Her *marchand* stopped by this morning; he has a gay lover who works for the government. He claimed to have seen Olinda's name on a hit list. Most of the names were of left-wing artists and intellectuals, but they also included footballers and boxers. Absurd, yet true; this is too frightening."Luigi sounded sombre.

"What is she going to do? She shouldn't stay here."Was the information provided by the art dealer's lover reliable?

"I think she's planning to go to her parents in Bom Jesus de Lapa. Her *marchand* seems to think that it's safer outside the big cities. Nowadays, her comrades from the Party seem to agree that she should leave."

"What a bloody mess!"Then, thinking of her invitation that morning, Daniel added, "We can all go to Wanda's parents!"

"It won't work,"said Luigi. "Olinda wants to be with her son; it's been a long time since she's seen him. I don't know whether to go with her or not."

The military in Brazil, just like their Argentinian counterparts, thought that they were the new Messiahs, destined to save the continent from the forces of evil and moral corruption. Meanwhile, the sense of chaos was deepening, unemployment was rising and inflation was completely out of control. Business deals were made in dollars, and always in cash. The abortionist wasn't the only one.

"It's happening everywhere: in Argentina, in Chile, in Uruguay, how do you explain it? Is the sun too hot in this part of the world? Do we eat too much meat?"

"We should piss off to Europe and let South America just sink into oblivion, nobody is going to miss it."

That kind of cynicism wasn't going to help. Just then, Olinda came through the door carrying a tray with a pot of coffee, cakes, cups and plates.

"Would you like some dessert?"

"We need something sweet,"said Luigi.

Olinda sat by Wanda and put a comforting arm around her.

Luigi cut the cakes and Daniel took charge of serving the coffee; as usual, it was sweet, rich, thick.

"I wonder if you'll like these cakes. This one, with meringue and almonds on top, is called *amor in pedaços* – love in pieces; the little puffed cakes are called *sonhos* – dreams,"explained Olinda. "We found them in the kitchen. Doña Teresinha must have brought them some time yesterday when we were out."

Daniel refused to tell them what he knew. He certainly didn't want to confess his uncanny experience of the previous day, when the old woman had appeared and disappeared as if by magic. Besides, he didn't want to tell them about Doña Teresinha's interest in his ass.

"You smell of bread."They were in bed. She liked to lie by his side, her head resting on his shoulder, hugging him like a bear.

"You read my hand once,"Wanda reminded him, "would you do something else?"

"Like what?'

"You said poets consult the I-Ching."

The things one says.

"Please, I would like to know my future."

"OK, tomorrow, we'll get the book from a library, or we'll buy one, I promise."He wasn't too sure that he wished to know his own future. The abortion, the news about Olinda, and Wanda's wish to see her father had unsettled him.

"How are you feeling?"

"All right, but in a bit of pain,"she admitted.

"I admire you, you're very brave."

"So, tell me, did you have goose or turkey for Christmas at home?"The Syrian's influence was there to stay.

"We didn't celebrate Christmas. Nevertheless, we usually got together for a meal, so as not to feel left out. But I got presents at Epiphany!'

Daniel remembered some of his own presents: a tin drum, a proper leather football, *El Estanciero*, the pirate costume. He looked forward to the arrival of the Three Wise Men more than his own birthday.

"And we had chicken."

"Did your mother also fatten the bird?'

Wanda didn't have any notion of where and how he had lived as a child.

"We lived in a very small flat at the back of my father's shop. My parents slept in one room with my little sisters. Then there was another room, with a collapsible dining table and two small beds, where I slept with my grandmother. The kitchen was tiny; only one person at a time could fit in it. No room for keeping chickens."

If there was any unhappiness in his childhood, it wasn't for lack of money or the absence of a car, or the restricted space at home. Even not having a TV to watch *I Love Lucy* or *Highway Patrol* didn't seem that much of a hardship.

"What kind of a shop did your father have? Did he sell sweets and chocolates?'

"He repaired and restored second-hand pianos."

"So you played the piano when you were a kid,"Wanda said, with interest.

"My first piano teacher was an old bag who made me cry at every lesson for not practising enough. With the best of intentions, my mother got another one, but she didn't work out either. From then on, I was provided with a series of attractive young girls who drove me mad with their perfume and their half-open blouses. But that wasn't all, I was sure that my father was fucking my piano teachers, one after another."

In an instant, Wanda's giggles gave way to tears.

"Why are you crying?"

"Because you're my friend."

"You're also my friend, Wanda."

"We'll never say *adeus* – goodbye. We'll only ever say *até logo* to each other,"she said. And then, "Since you're obviously

not going to sing me a tango tonight, and the reading of the
I-Ching has to be postponed, I have another request: recite a
poem for me."

Daniel was incapable of remembering any poetry by heart,
only fragments – except for Robert Desnos' last poem, found
written on a piece of paper in his pocket after he died. He told
Wanda that Desnos had been part of the Resistance, that he was
captured by the Germans when they occupied France and sent to
Büchenwald; that he died of typhus and malnutrition just after
the Allied liberation.

"What's Büchenwald?'

"A horrible place, Wanda. I'll tell you about it some other
time."

"OK, tell me the poem now."

Daniel lifted himself up, arranged the pillows against the wall
and leaned against them; Wanda stretched out against his legs,
her arms around his waist.

"This was dedicated to his wife, whose name was Youki."

I dreamed so much of you
I walked so much, talked so much
loved your shadow so much
that nothing of you is left for me.
All I can be is a shadow among shadows
be a hundred times more shadow than the shadow
be the shadow that will return and always return
to your life, full of sun.

Wanda turned around and pressed her back against his chest.
She then asked him to embrace her, to hold her breasts and kiss
her neck.

"One day, would you have a child with me?'

"Of course!'

"I'd like five,"she said.

PART III

1

Daniel, my dearest friend,
I'm writing this quick note on a sunny afternoon in La Giralda, one of the few places that still remains intact in our memory of the present. I think of you a lot – perhaps, I should confess, with a certain amount of envy. Things have suddenly turned sour for me. I'll explain it one day, it's not very complicated. It's all happening because of my involvement with the Union; to be a Communist is not easy. I have arranged for Laura and the kids to leave Argentina; tomorrow, they'll be crossing by the overnight ferry to Montevideo, and fly from there to Spain; we have some great friends, Chuchi and Horacio, who live in Sitges; they will be waiting for them in Barcelona. And I'll follow them soon.

I'll be sending you this letter with a French teacher on exchange, who is on his way back to Avignon; he'll post it at the airport in São Paulo. He and I have become good friends; last time we met at his house, he introduced me to French wine; the one I tasted was called Châteauneuf-du-Pape, it was très bon! It gave me hope: if there is wine like that in other places on earth, we don't need to live and die in Buenos Aires. In the last few weeks, Laura & I slept in separate places, changing addresses every night; the kids stayed in Quilmes, with my mother-in-law. Anyway, we can't stay in this country. I'm planning to stop in Rio on my way to Europe. If you can, write to me – to my mother's address, so I know how to find you. It'll be good to hear your voice, away from all this. I don't feel guilty any longer about wanting to leave. I'm not cut out to be a hero. Un abrazo y hasta pronto.

Chau,
Damián

2

It was raining in Rio. Olinda and Luigi had woken up early and gone out for a walk. She said the morning light inspired her to paint. Given the choice, Luigi would have stayed in bed longer, like Wanda and Daniel, and laze around the house. Nevertheless, Luigi always accompanied Olinda on these excursions; he too felt inspired during the walks. On their return to the house, he concentrated on his novel; Olinda, on her paintings.

On one of those long walks, Luigi had browsed in a secondhand bookshop and found a lifesize print of a parrot resembling Joacaría. They learnt from the notes on the drawing that Joacaría's scientific name was *Deropytus accipitrinus accipitrinus* (Linnaeus, 1758), better known by the vulgar name of *Anacã* or Red-fan Parrot. They lived in small bands, or in pairs during the breeding season, in the upper part of the Rio Negro. Their domain extended widely: Colombia, Ecuador, Peru, Venezuela, the Guyanas.

"I thought I detected a Colombian accent in him," Luigi said. Nobody paid any attention to him. "Whatever you wish, you all seem to know it all, but there is one thing that cannot be disputed: of all the keas, cockatoos, lories, parakeets, parrolets, budgerigars, lovebirds, conures, rosellas, cockatiels, lorikeets, amazons and macaws that you could find in the tropics, Joacaría is the most striking of them all."

"That's not what we're arguing about; you were talking about accents,"Olinda replied.

"I think there might be a strong link between the incomparable beauty of this bird and his Colombian accent,"Luigi insisted, but he didn't manage to convince them. "The problem is that none of you believe that Joacaría really talks, that he knows what he's saying. Do you think that he would be so affectionate if he didn't know how to talk? If I disappeared one day, he'd die of loneliness. "

"It isn't Joacaría's love for you that concerns me so much,"said Olinda, "but your crush on him. If only *he* was a girl."

Luigi himself probably shared Olinda's concern: he had the drawing framed and hung it near the parrot's perch, hoping that Joacaría would fall in love with it. A useless exercise: what Joacaría wanted was real human contact, mutual touching and kissing and scratching, not a printed image of his sister – or was it a brother?

On this rainy morning, while Olinda and Luigi were out walking, Daniel was woken by a loud banging at the front door. It was deafening and boomed through the whole house; somebody was hollering at the top of his voice, demanding that the door be opened.

It seemed to take ages for him to wake up. He was dreaming that he was in a park, no, it looked more like a French garden, a perfect example of ornamental landscaping surrounding a big, white chateau ... an abandoned mansion, its shutters closed, empty ponds, dirty terraces ... Was it from *Last Year in Marienbad*? He passed a greenhouse full of plants; someone was trying to hide in a corner behind the palm trees; a persistent call was urging him to run to the end of the path. Was he going to make it? It was then that he heard the banging and shouting, and woke up.

What was the time? He sat up and retrieved his watch from the floor. He looked at it, not being able to understand the simplest thing, for example that the watch was upside down, it was an effort to think of turning it right side up. "Coming, coming,"he muttered sluggishly. He turned around and looked at Wanda, complete in her sleep, head buried in the pillow, cut off from the noises of the world. "Sweet dreams, Wanda,"he smiled. He got up and started to walk the long corridor to the door, still thinking of *Marienbad*, reciting Antonio Machado's famous lines:

> *Walker, there are no roads*
> *Roads are made by walking...*

"What's the damn use of poetry?"he asked out loud. He never got a chance to answer this existential question. As soon as he opened the door, something hit him in the centre of his face – ten tons of cement landed on his teeth. He could still hear the referee counting out the seconds: "One, two, three..."No, he wasn't going to get up, no glory for him this time, the winner could take all the prize money, it didn't matter.

Once, he had trained at a gym behind Luna Park, full of young aspiring boxers who dreamed of world titles to be won at Madison Square Garden. It didn't last long: he couldn't even skip rope properly, let alone avoid the jabs, hooks and uppercuts that came his way.

How many times was the referee going to start the count again?

Sitting on the floor he contemplated the little white pieces in his hand; they were two hard triangles, fragments of teeth. The impact had made him bleed; feeling the warm sensation on his tongue, he tasted blood and was in no doubt as to who had been the owner of those teeth.

"What the fuck do you think you're doing?"the man at the door asked him. "You thought you could mess with me? Do you know who I am?'

"I don't fink we'f been introduthed,"Daniel barely mumbled. He was discovering what front teeth were for, was he going to talk like that for the rest of his life? From where he was sitting on the floor, the man looked enormous, a formidable butcher, a champion who won his fights by sheer brutal obstinacy.

"What are you looking at? You're still fucking with me? You Argentinian son of a bitch, you think you can come here and take what belongs to me? Just like that? Who do you think you are, you piece of crap?"

He was a mulatto Brylcreem boy, an Elvis Presley with flattened curls; he must have spent hours trying to straighten the kinks. Daniel could not believe he had knocked out his teeth that way. The blow was still echoing through his head, making it difficult to think.

"The bitch tried to cheat me, that's not good for business; it's taken me weeks to find her; I haven't risked my life to protect her from the bloody cops so the fucking whore could now think she can just quit; she still owes me money, just don't butt in, get it?'

"What do you want fom me?"Daniel asked. Clearly, Olinda and Luigi would not be home for a while, and Joacaría was nowhere to be seen. He only hoped Wanda wouldn't wake up. "Maybe I can crush his head with something hard,"he thought.

"I'll tell you what,"said the Brylcreem boy, "I'm a reasonable man, I don't mind you fucking her and living with her, you've got a nice setup here and she needs love and affection and I can't give it to her, so…'

Very fucking moving. Daniel wanted right there and then to blow the rat's brains out. At that point, something flew past Daniel's head and struck the beast on his left arm. Everything went silent. Then he exploded like a wounded animal: he yelled and howled, and his screams turned into a horrific barking. A small kitchen knife, the same one that Wanda and Daniel had used for peeling oranges in bed the previous night, was now stuck in the man's impressive biceps.

"I could have had your heart, you son of a bitch,"cried a fierce, homicidal Wanda. "This was just a warning; next time, I swear to God, I'll kill you, I promise before Jesus and Exú."

A double promise not to be ignored.

The pimp stood looking at the knife stuck in his arm, not believing what had happened to him. He didn't know what to do. He kept screaming, "Bitch! Bitch!"He dropped the knuckle-duster that he had been holding in his hand and took a handkerchief from a back pocket to stop the blood oozing down his arm. In fact, Daniel was surprised at how little blood there was. He was disappointed, and wished the pimp as much suffering as possible. He felt a certain satisfaction imagining the moment when the knife would be withdrawn from the arm, the serrated blade sawing on his flesh.

Despite her fury, Wanda seemed in control. She stepped forward and threw something else at the man, who lurched away, yelling a desperate "Nooo!"

"That settles the account, I owe you nothing, it's finished,"she declared. It was the rest of the American dollars that she'd used to pay the abortionist. The bundle hit the pimp lightly on the chest and fell to the floor. He bent over to pick it up, and rammed it into his pocket.

"This isn't the end, you fucking bitch!'

"Get this into your thick skull full of brick-dust: if you dare come near me again, I'll kill you. I don't want to see you ever again,"she yelled back.

The pimp opened the door, and slowly stepped out of the house without looking back.

Once the pimp left, Daniel ran towards her; he wanted to embrace her but she pulled away from him and went to fetch a bucket of water. Wanda started wiping the blood from the floor with a sponge and lots of detergent. "I'll do it! I'm responsible for this, I have to do it!"she kept repeating angrily whenever Daniel offered to help.

"What do you think is going to happen now?"he asked. Daniel wasn't sure how to talk to her or what to say; she kept pushing him away.

"I don't know,"she cried, "I don't know."Wanda repeated these words in a crescendo of pain and despair; she went on rubbing frantically at the spot where the pimp's blood had dripped. The floor was now clean. Gradually, the cleaning turned into a thumping of the wooden boards with clenched fists while her voice cracked into raging, shuddering sobs. Daniel knelt in front of her and took hold of her hands firmly, pulling her up from the floor.

"Stop it! Enough!"he shouted.

Wanda freed herself from his grasp and started beating him on the chest. The humiliation, the bitterness, the profound hatred that even Wanda herself was unaware of feeling, welled up and burst in a convulsion; all the blows she had suffered in life, the accumulated resentment took hold of her body and made her shake and cry. Daniel's determination won in the end; he was able to hold her tightly against his chest, enough to contain her. Wanda gave up struggling, her sobs subsided; then, she closed her eyes and passed out in his arms. Daniel lifted her up – so small, so fragile. He lay her on the sofa and covered her with a light blanket. Wanda opened her eyes and looked at him; she managed a faint smile.

"Where did you learn to throw a knife like that?"he asked softly.

"During my childhood, while waiting for my father to return from his trips to the jungle; I spent many afternoons throwing knives at the tree at the back of our garden, killing hundreds of imaginary enemies."

"Those afternoons paid off,"he said. Finally, after mumbling something incomprehensible, Wanda fell asleep.

Joacaría reappeared out of the blue at the end of the corridor. He walked almost on tiptoe, as if not wanting to wake Wanda, perhaps still wary of the pimp's presence. He had been hiding behind the towels on the open shelves next to the bathroom; now he came down the corridor muttering *"tramontane, tramontane..."*

"Sí, amigo, tramontane my foot."

The ruffian's visit was a tornado that had scrambled Daniel's brains. He could only afford one thought, "we have to get the hell out of here!"The pimp was bound to come back, and next time he wasn't going to be alone. It would probably get nastier, not the kind of game Daniel and his friends wanted to play. Nothing tied him to Rio; if Wanda wanted to visit her family, he would go with her. He was also convinced that he could persuade Olinda and Luigi to join them later in Manaus.

Daniel sat on a chair by the window, contemplating Wanda in her sleep. He remembered a couple of lines from a short story: "...who could give me the measure of things, if not your silent presence, your illuminated body?" Even in these circumstances, when erotic thoughts were out of place, Daniel felt a longing for Wanda's body. It was so peaceful, she was sleeping so placidly, nobody could have guessed what had happened a few minutes earlier. Even though the blow had only broken his teeth, Daniel ached all over, as if he'd gone the full fifteen rounds.

Joacaría, after drinking some water from his bowl, jumped up on Daniel's shoulder and started to groom his hair, which Daniel had decided to grow long. This show of affection was unusual: though the parrot was friendly to everyone in the house, so far he had only shown that kind of tenderness for Luigi. Undoubtedly, he had been badly affected by the uproar and wanted some consolation.

Daniel contemplated the two fragments of broken teeth and the knuckleduster, which he had placed together on top of the desk. The parrot suddenly stopped his activities and became tense and agitated. He jumped from Daniel's shoulder onto the desk, climbing from there onto his perch. By nature, Joacaría depended on the use of both legs to feed himself. After the replacement of one of his legs by a small hardwood stick, Joacaría had immediately discovered that if he lifted the good leg to hold nuts and chunks of banana, papaya and corn, he would fall over; the wooden leg didn't offer him sufficient balance to hold his feeding position. This improved slightly with the passing of time, but since he was getting very thin and obviously wasn't eating well enough, Luigi had decided to build a special platform on one half of the bird's perch. He bored little holes in its surface, which allowed Joacaría to stick his wooden leg into them to keep his balance, freeing the good claw to hold food.

Joacaría was restless, and Daniel was alarmed when he heard noises outside the door; he expected the pimp to return, but not that soon. Maybe his henchmen had been waiting outside, somewhere in a car parked nearby. It took him a while to recognise Olinda and Luigi's voices; they were approaching the flat, arguing as usual. He looked at Joacaría in relief, but the bird avoided his eyes.

"You look guilty,"he laughed. And then as he was getting up, he whispered, "Well, you have nothing to hide."

As soon as they came in, Daniel waved at them to keep quiet, pointed to Wanda on the sofa, then herded them into the kitchen. He told them about the morning's events, giving a specially detailed account of how the knife had penetrated the flesh of the beast.

"Shit!"was Luigi's only comment. "So that's where the blood on the pavement came from."

Wanda appeared through the door, like an apparition. Olinda ran up to her and embraced her, consoling her. They stood together in the middle of the kitchen for a long while. Luigi pushed himself up to sit on the counter by the sink, observing them. Daniel sat at the table; he lit a cigarette and immediately put it out. Olinda and Wanda seemed to float in the air, their bodies in silhouette against the midday light filtering through the kitchen window. They could have been lovers.

"Shall I reheat the coffee?"asked Luigi jumping down from the counter.

"Shouldn't we take up the offer of your Spanish friend to move into her house in Recreio dos Bandeirantes?"Daniel asked Olinda.

"Too late,"said Olinda. "She left the country, went to Europe; her own son has gone underground, apparently, got involved with some Trotskyists at the Catholic University. Why don't we go to Cuba? The Party can really help me with this one. What are we doing here anyway? We know it's true, things can only get worse, why stay? I'd only have to go and fetch David."

Beneath her enthusiasm, one could easily see how distraught Olinda was. If her *marchand*'s lover had told the truth and his information was reliable, her life was in real danger. Who was going to protect her? Her friends were powerless. Who to go to? Olinda's comrades were well organised, but she didn't entirely trust them. The police? They were the ones behind the disappearances and the killings. Leaving the country wasn't such a bad idea, but Cuba seemed very far away. A few months ago, Daniel might have jumped at the idea of joining the revolution in the tropics; now, it had lost its appeal.

Olinda poured the coffee. Everybody was subdued. She picked up a book from the table. "I wish life were simpler,"she exclaimed, and opening the book she read out loud, "I was reading Rosa Luxemburg, all she ever wanted was a little room, perhaps a library of their own, regular work that would pay for the bills, an opera from time to time, a small circle of friends who can sometimes be asked to dinner…, it isn't much to ask for, is it?'

"Who was that, did you say?"asked Daniel.

"Rosa Luxemburg, in a letter to Jogiches, her lover,"explained Olinda. The book had been a birthday present from her *marchand*; the Party would not have approved.

Wanda cut in. "I want to go home, I just want to go home."

They felt silent – until a knock at the front door jolted them. Maybe, it would be the police and not the pimp this time. What a choice! Laurel and Hardy, or the tropical Brylcreem boy.

"Things come in threes,"Luigi said. First, the police; then, the pimp. Now what?

Didn't the abortion count? Daniel wondered.

It was Olinda who reacted; she walked towards the door, and the others followed anxiously. "Who is it?"she shouted without opening it.

"Telegram, *senhorita*,"announced the voice from outside. "From Argentina."

Daniel identified the smell instantly. His mother had made him carry a little square tablet of a white crystalline substance next to his chest for a whole year when he was in primary school. The Plague had arrived to his neighbourhood. In one of his Sunday morning sermons, the local priest maintained it was a Divine punishment for all the sexual sins his parishioners had committed. Porota, the spinster, a devout seamstress who lived down the road from Daniel's family, was found dead the following day. She had hanged herself, leaving a brief note on her sewing machine: "Oh God, forgive me, I have sinned with another woman."Her death didn't seem to move the Higher Authorities: every week more cases of polio were reported.

That whole year, to walk the five blocks that separated home from school became a nightmare. Daniel was terrified that the Plague could pounce on him at any corner. "Had he sinned?"he often asked himself after hearing from his friends about the sermon. *La Polio* could have been lying in wait for him behind any tree, under a parked car, in the tram that passed the corner of calle

Gurruchaga. He tried to spend as little time as possible in the school playground; he avoided getting near unknown children, but even his own friends could have been carrying it. That summer, public swimming pools also became forbidden territory: scientists had proved it was in the water as much as in the air.

So when his mother provided him with the tablet, his view of the world changed – he felt safe again. She had put the pungent substance into a small bag of white material, and hung it around his neck with a string. His mother proclaimed, "This, which I have sewn myself, will keep that *dreck* away."So there was Daniel, walking around smelling like a pharmacy. It took some time for him to realise that every other kid also had a similar, equally useless little bag under his shirt.

His grandmother told Daniel that it was also the remedy for angina and haemorrhages, for insomnia and indigestion, for piles and unwanted pregnancies – the one and only time that he had heard his grandmother mention anything related to sex. Camphor seemed to be threatening the very existence of doctors. He even found a couple of tablets inside his pillow; it would protect him, his grandmother claimed, from evil thoughts. The thoughts never stopped but he knew then that, if he had to die in his sleep, it would be a fragrant death.

The smell of camphor evoked by the telegram was overpowering; he couldn't tell his friends that Death was lurking, lying in wait somewhere in the house. Disconcerted, invaded by childhood memories, for a few seconds Daniel didn't know where he was. Luigi took the brief telegram from his hands and read it out loud: "*Papá-heart-attack-please-ring-urgent-colaciónese-Mamá.*"

"Let's ring your mother,"Luigi said.

Daniel agreed, but he couldn't move. He looked at Wanda, who was standing beside him; she moved closer and stroked his head. Her presence, and the contact of her hand made the smell of camphor disappear.

"It's only a heart attack,"Wanda said. "He hasn't died yet, look at my father, people have seven lives, you know – like cats."

"Or parrots,"he joked sadly. He had always thought that certain things could never happen to him: floods, earthquakes, wars. These happened somewhere else, far away, in distant countries, to other people. The death of a parent, something that could only happen once, at the most twice in somebody's life, *that* happened to other people, not to him. And Wanda was surely right, his father hadn't died yet.

Luigi was lucky: he got the operator to reach Daniel's mother straight away. It worked! – a small miracle.

"You sound funny,"said his mother by way of greeting him. He counted to ten. He could have explained: "Well, yes, you see, I fell in love with a whore, she's a *mulata* and very beautiful, and has a pimp who happened to knock half of my front teeth out in a fight; it wasn't even a fight, though in fact my lover stuck a small kitchen knife in the beast's biceps, and now I've just found out about Dad ..."

No, it wouldn't work.

"What happened?"he managed to ask before she said anything else.

"Are you OK?"There was no winning with her.

"Yes,"he said a bit impatiently. "Just tell me what happened to *papá.*"

"He was working in Córdoba, in Río Cuarto, when he had a heart attack. I got a telephone call from the hospital where he was taken by Juan Carlos, who was travelling with him; it's a private clinic, how are we going to pay for it?'

"We'll sort it out somehow."It was true, how were they going to pay a large medical bill?

"He seems to be in a stable condition, I'd like you to come home, is that possible? Or are you very busy? When can you get here?'

"I'll have to find out about the flights."

"And don't worry."

"Please, *mamá*."

There was a pause.

"How are you?"his mother finally asked. This time she meant it.

"I'm fine, how about you?'

"We all miss you ... and I ... I'm scared."

What did *colaciónese* mean? Instead of saying *telegrama*, one said *colacionado*. At the end of every telegram, there it was, that word: *colaciónese*. Once, he had looked it up in the dictionary: the definition made no sense. *Colacionar* was to compare or collate, to bestow an ecclesiastical benefice or a university degree. He had always loved his *Pequeño Larousse Ilustrado*, with its coloured flags from all the countries in the world on the inside cover – including one for the Olympic Games and another for the United Nations. He loved the flags of Malawi and Kenya, admired those of Lebanon and Tunisia, and thought that the ones for Poland and Monaco were the most boring. Germany's flag, of course, he found the most aggressive and despicable. Daniel spent hours studying the pink pages of the dictionary, trying to memorise the Latin and Foreign Expressions. Those pages divided the book in two distinct sections: One was Language, the other, Art, Literature, Science. The pink pages were his favourite ones, located almost in the middle, perfectly dividing two different worlds. After all those years he could only remember two expressions: *Omnia mecum porto*, and *Le style c'est l'homme*.

He was having to leave Brazil so suddenly, prematurely. He didn't feel ready to go, to leave Wanda, not to know when -if ever- he was going to see her again. The news about his father had left him cold. After the first thunderbolt and the unsettling smell of camphor, his body felt anaesthetised, his mind dazed. He had also been disturbed by a thought: although he didn't have any clear notion of what could happen to a person after a heart attack, he wished his father would die rather than survive as an invalid. From this intolerable thought he leapt to another, equally horrible: "if my father dies, I'll feel freer'. He felt a bit crazy. Sitting on the sofa, still in shock, he murmured: "*Omnia mecum porto...*'

"What?"asked Luigi.

"'Everything I possess, I carry with me." Famous words, uttered by Bias in leaving the city of Pryene. It's in Latin, but it came from Greece, who knows why? It was in the *Pequeño Larousse Ilustrado*, that's all I know."

Luigi was sitting on the floor, with Joacaría perching on his shoulder. Daniel thought that he would go back to Argentina by himself; Luigi would stay behind with the two women and the bird; he would rejoin them as soon as possible – wherever. But Luigi was adamant: he was going back to Argentina with him. No arguments.

The Argentinian military government had cancelled all the concessions for civilians to travel on military planes. Luigi had begged and in the end had even got angry over the phone with the Consulate. No luck. The only possibility was to travel by bus. Luigi's decision had surprised them all, but Daniel was obviously relieved and grateful. He hated the idea of making such a long journey alone.

"I read the *Larousse* four or five times when I was a kid,"Luigi announced. "Sixty thousand entries, five thousand illustrations in black and white, a hundred maps. The best was the *Larousse* logo: a girl blowing seeds in the wind, with the words *Je sème à tout vent* encircling her; beneath the logo was printed what I thought was her address: 17, Rue du Montparnasse, Paris. One day, I thought, I'll get there...'

Dinner was a subdued, rather tense affair. Olinda burned the rice, and the beans were only half-cooked. Nobody seemed to care very much; food was the last thing on their minds. For the first time in a long while, Joacaría was talking to himself in a soft, almost inaudible voice, oblivious to the people around him. Luigi tried without much enthusiasm to engage the bird, first in conversation, and failing that, in a cuddling session. Joacaría didn't respond. He was simply lost in his own world, gibbering away on his perch by the window.

Daniel didn't know how to reconnect with Wanda; he was also lost in his world. The fantasy that they had shared just a few hours before – the idea of meeting in Manaus – had collapsed with the arrival of the telegram. Now, Daniel was leaving, and Luigi had offered to go with him. Maybe Wanda was thinking that they would never see each other again. Or was that what he himself feared? He was troubled by his reaction to the telegram: had he actually smelled the camphor? It must have been a hallucination. Was this the result of too much *maconha*? They had been smoking almost every day; was his brain beginning to dissolve under the effect of the drug? And then there was Damián's letter. Now, he was leaving the country. At a distance, everything seemed a bit exaggerated. Daniel had to go back to see his father and take care of his mother and his sisters, no question about it. Would he be in danger too?

"What are you thinking?" asked Luigi.

"About smells ..." Daniel responded. Olinda giggled nervously, Wanda and Luigi looked at him puzzled. He explained what had happened with the camphor.

"I had completely forgotten about it!" Luigi exclaimed. "You're right, everybody was carrying that stuff."

"And then you criticised me for believing in *Macumba*," Olinda said.

"I wonder what it is about smells," Luigi continued. "When I was at the seminary, I was terrified that the priests could smell the sperm through the odours emanating from my hands after masturbating. The priests called it "self-defilement"; I didn't know what they were talking about for a long time; finally it dawned on me that they meant wanking, the greatest sin. The fact that at night we all made the beds shake like trampolines didn't change my vision of inevitable damnation. I couldn't even tell my confessor about my energetic practices. There was no way to escape my destiny: I was buying a one-way ticket."

Luigi was unstoppable: "One of the priests was truly mad: he went around sniffing everyone. He was convinced that the semen that remained in the body could go off, like yoghurt gone sour. He demanded that the semen should be extracted in some artificial way from the youngsters, before it poisoned their bodies. He suggested it could all be collected in a container, stored in the basement, and then be added to the fertilisers for the vegetable garden. The problem was, of course, how to collect it without the procedure giving too much pleasure. Poor Padre Bernardo! He was finally confined to a solitary cell at the top of the monastery, locked up for the rest of his days with a Bible and a chamber-pot as his only companions."

He added: "At the time of the polio epidemic, my parents followed the advice of our family doctor: "Take your child to the seaside; the strong, salty air will protect him.""And smiling at Olinda, he declared, "There you have it, another piece of bullshit! So we moved for three months to Mar del Plata -the happiest months of my life. Nothing to do with the sea, of course, it was being away from school that did me good, playing the whole time on those huge beaches."

Suddenly, the panther came out of her lair. "You don't have good beaches anyway, what good could that cold Southern Atlantic have done? Nothing, fuck all, nothing! Beaches? You want some beaches? I'll give you beaches: Pituba, Armaçâo, Piatâ, Placaford, Itapoâ, Subaúma, Suipé, Palame, Barra de Itariri, Mangue Seco ... And the ones in San Salvador? Arraial D'Ajuda, Pitinga, Mucugê, Taipe, Rio da Barra, Trancoso ... Or maybe Paixâo, Tororâo, Areia Preta, Cumuruxatiba ... These are beaches for real people, for real men, not pansies."What had happened? Where had she smelt warm blood? She was ready to pounce on her prey. "I would take you to Alagoas and show you what paradise really is, where the waters are blue and the air is clear and people actually love each other: Pajuçara, Sete Coqueiros, Ponta Verde, Jatiúca, Jacarecica, Guaxuma, Carça Torta, Riacho Doce, Pratagi...'

Mad with rage, Wanda spat out the words with the same precision she had used to throw the knife, her speech turning into a passionate and furious lesson in Brazilian geography. As a diatribe it made little sense, but they all understood.

At that instant, the floodgates unexpectedly broke: Daniel felt as if something had been injected into his veins; the warmth of a powerful drug invaded his body and the numbness disappeared. "How can she be so unconditionally admirable?" he thought. If only he would get another telegram, some fresh piece of news that would turn the clock back.

And if he took her with him?

And if he married her?

That night, Wanda and Daniel were both exhausted but alert. He had been the first to leave the gathering in the kitchen – he had exceeded his quota of *caipirinhas*. Wanda followed him to their bedroom later. Lying in bed, smoking a cigarette, the lights turned off, Daniel contemplated Wanda taking off her clothes in the gloom, her dark skin shining in the shadows. She sat beside him on the edge of the bed, and slowly finished undoing the buttons of her blouse.

"I'm sorry about your father, I can imagine what you feel. And I'm also sorry about being so angry, all that stupid stuff about the beaches."

"It's OK."He wanted to tell her about his numbness, he would have liked to explain that he understood her reaction, to mention the distance between them, to say something about the uncertainty of their future.

"Would you like complete service, *monsieur*?'

"Wanda, please."

"No names, mister, the house doesn't allow personal relationships between workers and clients."

He had felt very uneasy on a previous occasion when Wanda played the whore. She was obviously freer than he was to play that game. Yes, uneasy -but he didn't dislike it.

They could hear screeches and groans and hoots and grunts and wails coming from the jungle below.

"The whole orchestra is out tonight."

"It's the full moon, it brings the beasts out, didn't you notice my fangs, sir? I'm wearing my serpent's venom-tooth."She showed her teeth, which reflected the light coming through the window, and pretended she was a vampire. "You won't even have to tip me extra for this."Wanda proceeded to undo his jeans, and then pulled down his underwear. She held his penis between her hands, reviving it with her caresses. Daniel held her by the shoulders and forced her on top of him. They kissed. He felt he would have liked to fill and satisfy every orifice in her body, to make her feel complete. Yet, in the middle of their passionate embrace, he thought, "What a way to celebrate your father's heart attack!" It lasted a fraction of a second, not enough to spoil it. Nevertheless, it made him wonder: how could anybody be in two places at once? Weird.

"What is it?"Wanda had registered it.

"Nothing,"Daniel murmured.

"You know, I'd never fucked anybody who had been clipped."

"How, clipped?'

"Clipped, like yours, did it hurt when they did it?'

"You mean circumcised!'

"Yes, did it hurt?"

To each his own madness.

"I don't know, I was a few days old."

She started moving slowly, while he held her buttocks firmly, as if trying to stop her. She bit him hard and made him squeal. "My venom is harmless,"she laughed.

He was now on top of her, he could see her face clearly in the moonlight.

"Wanda ...'

"What?'

"Would you like to marry me?"

There it was, he'd said it. Such madness!

Wanda's body stopped moving, she rolled to one side, and there she remained, silent for a long while. Daniel daren't say anything else; he just waited, feeling awkward, inadequate, wondering if he had offended her with his suggestion. What was she thinking? Then, she whispered, "It's the best present you could have given me, but I won't marry you or anybody else. *"Mundo mundo vasto mundo..."* Do you remember? We read that poem together, once."

Of course he remembered!

"Look, we could make up another version of the poem:

> *World, world, vast world,*
> *If my name was Raimundo*
> *It wouldn't just be a rhyme,*
> *It would be a solution!'*

Daniel had meant it, but Wanda had more common sense than he did. How on earth she could have said yes? His proposal was not a solution.

"Look now, there's a job to be done, so get on with it, don't try to find excuses,"They pressed hard against each other. "I need sugar in my bowl, don't distract me."

""Sugar in my bowl"? Is that what you said? I didn't think you knew Bessie Smith."

"Who's Bessie Smith?'

"A blues singer, she's the one who sings of having sugar in her bowl'.

"I don't know her, I just heard it in a romantic soap on TV."

"You and your soaps."

From then on they didn't talk any more. They settled to their task with slow, unequivocal pleasure. They had learnt to respect their different rhythms, the waves that brought them together, the currents that pulled them apart. Each of them had shown a mutual curiosity for the different messages conveyed by their bodies. They had come to trust each other; whatever happened, however many detours each of them took, they both knew they would meet in the end. It was a simple formula: they gave as much as they took. They brewed their own home-made magic potion which had always made them happy, and – at times – extremely happy. Given the circumstances, that night could have been sad, but never solemn. Finally, they both fell asleep.

He didn't expect to but he woke soon after. Neither of them had said a word about his imminent departure. Maybe it was better that way. Now awake, he thought of his father; with his eyes closed, he tried to remember his face, but it was Damián's face that kept reappearing. He decided to get up and had a long shower. When he walked into the kitchen, he was surprised to see Luigi there, scribbling some notes. Daniel sat across from him. Luigi confessed his wish to write a story about Rio, and Daniel helped him to record some of the events of the last few weeks. They both had a bad headache, were tired and hungover. From the only window in the kitchen, all they could see was the dirty wall of the inside patio. They heard the radio announcing the latest soccer results, warning of a tropical storm, high winds, heavy rain.

"What's going to happen with Joacaría? He's going to suffer."

"Olinda gave him to me, she says he's mine now, I'm taking him with us," Luigi said, trying hard to make it sound like a casual remark.

"Who?'

"Joacaría."

"Where?'

"To Buenos Aires."

"How?'

"I'm doping him. I've spoken to the vet on the phone, he recommended some barbiturates. In fact, he'll give me some free samples; he says the capsules are slow-release, each lasts for about eight hours; six of them will be more than enough to keep Joacaría asleep and dopey long enough to get to Buenos Aires. Don't worry about it, everything is under control."

"We're all nuts."It would have been useless to argue. "And where are you going to carry this poor parrot?'

"I'm borrowing a big baggy jacket from Olinda, I'll carry him in one of the inside pockets."

"What if he needs to take a shit?'

Luigi looked stupefied; he hadn't thought of that possibility.

"He won't have to take a shit,"he declared, once he had recovered. "I'll talk to him."

It was Wanda's idea: she booked two places on a bus going north; the two women had decided to leave – nothing was keeping them. Olinda would join her son and her family; and Wanda was to meet her father at his house by the Rio Negro, just outside Manaus, for their long-overdue reconciliation. They had made sure to choose a bus that would leave very early; Wanda wanted Luigi and Daniel to see them off. She didn't want to feel that Daniel was leaving her.

At the bus terminal, Daniel gave each of the women a prolonged kiss on the mouth; Luigi did the same. And then, more hugs and more kisses; the ceremony lasted a long while, what with jokes, sobs and reminiscences of the good times. Then, when it was no longer possible to postpone the departure, the two men stood on the platform, waving to Olinda and Wanda, who were crying on the bus while shouting at the same time *ciao!* and *arrivederci, tutti quanti!* – as if they were all Italians. Finally, the bus drove off. Daniel and Luigi went back into the terminal. Daniel disappeared to the toilets, while Luigi went to fetch their tickets from the counter.

Upon his return, Daniel didn't recognise the man standing beside Luigi.

"Your friend here,"the man said, pointing to Luigi, "has told me about the death of your father. I'm sorry."

Was he, really? Why? For a few seconds, the man's affected voice made him think of Leandro Cabral –el Señor Sotana, from the Bar Lua, back from the beyond. It wasn't him. This guy was shorter and stockier, dressed in studied informal clothes, an impeccable white cotton shirt and black linen trousers. He had a beard, which he kept well trimmed. He looked cool but Daniel thought he was a creep.

"I appreciate your concern,"Daniel responded. What else?

"Salvador Narciso do Pouço', the guy introduced himself.

"I am Daniel,"he said, keeping it brief. "And what brought you here, to this terminal? Where are you journeying?"Now he was imitating him.

"I came to find out about the bus route to Ushuaia, I'm moving there."He was serious.

"Why?"Daniel was genuinely curious.

"I've seen the light!'

"Oh, yes?'

"It happened just after my first visit to an Indian guru."

"You don't say."

"In fact, he originally came from Pakistan… a prince!'

"How interesting!'

"As soon as I saw him, so attractive the man, I felt transfixed by his penetrating look. He told me straight, "the problem with you, Salvador, is that you're a bullshitter". He also said that I kept on re-writing my history -past, present and future; that I was *un mitomane*.

He said it in French! I felt very proud. It was a revelation."
    "So, what did you say?'
    "Such insight! What a mind! Such an honest man! I'd
been moaning for the last few years that I haven't been really
recognised for what I really am. In telling me the truth about my
self, this great man gave me that opportunity to do something
special with my life. I will now prove myself, I will be recognised
by my colleagues and friends."
    "But, in Ushuaia? Why so far away?'
    "Ushuaia needs analysts, the provincial government made me
an offer I couldn't refuse."
    "What kind of analysts?'
    "Chemical analysts."
    "What do you do?
    "I study and ascertain the chemical constitution of
substances."
    "Such as?'
    "Difficult to explain, just to give you an example: urban
waste, all sorts, for example, industrial refuse, domestic litter,
abandoned junk, in other words, general waste, including faecal
products."
    "Fascinating!"
    Luigi looked on; he was having a ball.
    "Indeed. I will be working for the Ministry of Public
Health…'
    Daniel interrupted him. Their bus was about to leave, its
engine running. Without much ceremony, they said goodbye.
    Once on the bus, Luigi, shaking his head, declared, "It takes
all kinds."

PART IV

1

Joacaría, Luigi and Daniel, without exchanging a word, dozed fitfully, enduring at first the heat of the day and then the chill at night -until they reached the South. The sudden braking of the bus woke them up again.

"I will always return to the South,"Daniel announced, yawning.

It was early in the morning, cold and very bright. They felt as if they could almost touch the deep blue sky with their fingertips, it seemed so near. They hadn't taken enough warm clothing, but Luigi was better off; he wore the jacket borrowed from Olinda and kept Joacaría in the inside pocket, against his chest.

For breakfast, they bought a couple of beers at a kiosk by the road and then drank some black coffee with brandy at a hotel. Under the long line of palm trees that separated them from the recently burnt cane fields, Luigi said, "We'll never get there."

They had travelled for many long hours and had only made it as far as Rio Grande do Sul. The bus, old and rickety, squeaked and rattled as it made its way. The red earth made all other colours look much brighter. Once they entered Porto Alegre, they were struck by the many fair-haired people everywhere, descendants of Germans, or maybe Swedes. At the restaurant next to the terminal they ordered sausages and a couple of beers. Yes, the *steinegger* and the thick *weisswurst* revealed the origins of the people. Strong, spicy food to revive the dead.

Luigi found a copy of the *Folha de São Paulo* at the newsstand. Luigi insisted on reading Daniel bits of national and international news. The governments of Latin America saw communists everywhere. Daniel couldn't feel too much interest. He had only one thought: would his father still be alive? Would he get there in time? The hours seemed to lengthen interminably. Rio started to be a dream in the distant past, and Wanda appeared in his thoughts like a mythical figure. Just a few hours ago he had known what blouse she was wearing, he could recognise the smell of her curly hair, the scent of her body, her unmistakable laugh, all kinds of trivial details of their daily existence. Now, she had become inaccessible, unfathomable, he was making efforts to recall her face. Memory was a trickster.

"I'm dying for a *mate*,"Daniel said. "I'd like to get some sleep, do you have any sedatives to spare?'

Joacaría had managed well and remained quiet inside Olinda's jacket. Luigi had mixed a reduced dose of the medicine with sugar water at the start of the trip; he made Joacaría drink it with a dropper he bought at the chemist. From time to time, a soft muttering could be heard, registering a complaint, but Joacaría seemed to have understood what was required of him.

Luigi produced a free sample of a clear capsule filled with tiny dark blue, pale blue, and white pellets. Daniel put the capsule on his tongue and swallowed it with a gulp of water. There was an explanatory leaflet inside the small box: *"For the treatment of epilepsy, and in conditions requiring continuous sedation ...'*

"Epilepsy? Perfect, just for me! This should do me good."Daniel continued reading: *""Patients should be instructed to avoid alcohol while under treatment..."* We had two beers and a brandy."

"This is supposed to sedate you, not make you more anxious. Don't worry about it, enjoy your dreams, dope fiend."

Once back on the bus, Daniel didn't feel too well. He was fighting against sleep, trying unsuccessfully to read one of the books they had brought with them. Despite feeling dizzy, walking through clouds, he was quite pleased to get stoned on a legal drug. What was the attraction of books? His own parents never read them; his father bought the *Readers' Digest*, which Daniel suspected was left on the bedside table for the whole month, unread except for the jokes. Daniel himself had started his literary career with weekly comics: *Rayo Rojo*; *Misterix*; *El Pato Donald*. They were followed by abridged Westerns. It was a mystery how, at a very early age, he had developed a taste for the Republican poets of the Spanish Civil War. Where did he get them from? Oh, yes, now he remembered. Damián had showed him some of Antonio Machado's poems. Then, Federico García Lorca, Miguel Hernández, León Felipe. When he was older, the love for books led him to the shops on calle Corrientes, open until three in the morning. Later on, Luigi and Daniel had lived in a *pensión* just above the old restaurant La Emiliana. They ended many nights by having breakfast with *chocolate con churros* at the bar La Giralda, talking about Nietszche, the dialectics of the master–slave relationship, and the improbable existence of the Super Vagina described by Henry Miller.

"I wish I hadn't lost my ear in the war..." Daniel thought. He woke himself up with a jolt. Where had that thought come from? What was he dreaming about? His ear? What war? He couldn't figure it out. Ah, yes, books... Reading had come before writing; no, that wasn't true, writing came first. "But it was reading which saved me from going mad," he thought.

He fell into a heavy sleep.

They had to change buses, this time in Montevideo. Once in Colonia, they didn't have to wait long: the next ferry for Buenos

Aires was ready to depart. Luigi was silent, gently and lovingly pressing his jacket against his chest.

"This medication can't be that good for a poor parrot," Daniel thought, "it would probably knock out a cart-horse." No wonder Joacaría was behaving well.

The crossing was quick; the afternoon wind hadn't risen yet and the brown, contaminated waters of the River Plate were calm. The sun was shining, it was a glorious afternoon. Daniel wondered around the boat, absorbed in his own thoughts. He sat on a bench on the deck, remembering that other crossing to the Ilha de Paquetá. He thought of Eugenio, of his tragic destiny. There was no crime without a motive, why had he been killed? The police suspected a vendetta, and spoke of criminals wanting to "square an account" for a large amount of money owed for drugs. Daniel didn't believe a word of it; it couldn't have been drugs, there was nothing in their encounter with Eugenio at the Consulate which could have suggested it. Had he really been in so much debt? Eugenio didn't look like a junkie, and of course he wasn't a pusher. He was a poor sod, tormented by the ghosts in his house painted red and black to show his sympathy for the Devil. Had he been involved in something unimaginable? All that business about Exú and his wish to vindicate the deity's name. He also recalled the days spent at the black transvestites' flat, their arguments about religion, their meals together, the Carmen Miranda clothes, the unforgettable evening at the Festival do Escritor Brasileiro. He remembered the story of Socrates' change of name to Carmela, the Pantanal and Marie-Antoinette; the thick, hard turd on top of the white Mercedes Benz.

The engine's sudden change of pitch interrupted his thoughts: they had arrived.

The first encounter with the Argentinian authorities brought them thudding down to earth. While Luigi and Joacaría swiftly went through customs, Daniel was stopped by an immigration officer sporting a moustache like a Mexican bandit. "You can't go through,"the young man announced with almost orgasmic satisfaction; his job gave him the chance to exercise a little power. Daniel looked at him without registering his words. Or was he still under the influence of the sedative?

"Do I speak Chinese, *señor*? Or what?"One had to actually hear those words, pronounced in an unrelenting *porteño* accent, to understand their effect. Daniel was paralysed with indignation. In an absent way, he was thinking, "I'm going to kill him, I just have to grab his tie and pull it hard and long enough to strangle him, it's not difficult at all, I can do it, just let him finish, smile in the meantime".

Instead, he asked politely: "Could you tell me *why* you can't let me through?'

"The photograph, the photograph ..."the Abominable Bastard explained, pointing to his passport.

"What's the matter with it?"

"*Pero señor*, you've got a beard! There is none of that in the photograph!"

"But isn't it obvious from here to the most remote and unreachable mountains of China that the guy in the photo is none other that my own, unique, unsurpassed, unusual and ugly self. Can't you recognise me?"People in the queue behind him giggled.

"Not so many laughs, *señores*, not so many laughs,"said the man, leaning to one side so everybody could see him. He had grown impatient; he gave the passport back to Daniel with an abrupt gesture: "There is nothing I can do."That was it. " Let's see, next!'

"And if I shaved?"Daniel couldn't understand how he had come to think of it – for a moment he had felt completely lost. It even surprised the bureaucrat; he took his time to digest Daniel's suggestion. It was so obvious and simple.

"In that case, *sí*, no problem."

He couldn't believe it.

Luigi was safely on the other side of the glass panel, not knowing whether to laugh or cry.

"I'll be back in a minute."

He ran to the men's toilet. He cut his beard off with the scissors from his pocket-knife and shaved himself clean with his razor. He came out renewed, but by the time he made it back to the queue, the Mexican bandit had gone; a colleague of his now replaced him. Daniel was outraged; the son of a bitch didn't even give him that satisfaction.

Soon after, they were on yet another bus. "My ass feels square and flat from travelling so long on this shit,"he complained. They were home, and they weren't happy.

On the same day they arrived in Buenos Aires, Daniel's mother returned from Río Cuarto, where his father was hospitalised. With borrowed money, she had bought a plane ticket for Daniel to go and see him. Luigi, for his part, left straight away for Sierra de la Ventana, where his family now lived; he was planning to stay there for a while. They arranged to meet up later on in Buenos Aires to decide what to do next, how to plan their return to Rio.

"What happened to your teeth?', asked her mother intently.

"It's nothing, just a stupid accident, it doesn't hurt."At least, he didn't have to talk silly any longer; he had learnt to manage without his front teeth.

"I have something awful to tell you', her mother said. Daniel immediately realised: this wasn't about his father. It was something else. "I'm so, so sorry, your friend Damián has been murdered."

An uncanny chill went through his body. Murdered, no need to specify by whom.

"Oh, no! No! No! How? Why? When did you hear about it? He was supposed to have left the country."

"He was arrested in the middle of the night and taken to the Sección Especial of the Police Department; he was picked up on his way home after a Teachers' Union meeting,"explained his mother.

They had driven him away, a hood on his head, in a Ford Falcon; after a few hours at the calle Moreno, they moved him to an unknown destination. He was made to lie naked on a table. Playing a recording of the National Anthem at full volume to hide his screams, they applied *la picana* to his testicles, to the inside of his mouth, to his underarms. Afterwards, he had been left for dead on the road. He was found by some workers and taken to hospital; Damián had survived long enough to tell his mother what had happened.

"I'm worried about her, they will want to shut her up, she needs to be careful."Absolutely right. If Damián's mother was kicking up a fuss, the bastards might get her as well. They just didn't care.

"This is for being a Bolshevik sonofabitch," they told Damián as they tortured him. In the end, they threw him out onto the Panamericana highway in the middle of the night. Workers repairing the phone lines found him the next morning. His mother called a press conference but the papers barely mentioned the case. The police even suggested that he could have been attacked by his own party comrades, that Damián had quarrelled with the Central Committee of the CP, that he was a Trotskyist, that he was a delinquent.

Horrible. Unjust. A futile death.

Everything felt too fragile. Daniel had been trying to prepare himself to face his father's heart attack, but not this, his friend's death. It was all too much, how to take it all in? He felt devastated and confused. And yet, what to do? He had to move on. He spent most of the night speaking with his sisters and took the plane for Río Cuarto at dawn.

The brochure that Daniel picked up at the airport on arrival stated:

The city, the metropolis, the town, the village, constitute the initial
nucleus of a form of human social life that prolongs the intimate
life of the natal home, making us feel "us" by birth, residence,
and participation in a similar yearning for universal nobility.
According to Platonic philosophy, the City is not so much filled
with those aspects of its buildings that make it comfortable and
beautiful, but embodies a spirit, a morality, an education, a feeling
that does not negate material riches, but indeed establishes a set of
values ordered according to their priority for intimacy and living
together with others...

"What prose! What beauty! *Le style c'est l'homme.*"

He didn't have to wait for his luggage – he had brought
only a change of clothes in a plastic bag. He was first in line
at the taxi rank; he got in and gave the driver the name of the
hospital.

"Visiting relatives? I hope it's nothing serious."Not that the
man cared. "If you have time, don't miss a visit to the Parque
Sarmiento and the Anfiteatro, we even have a Museo de Bellas
Artes, this is a very cultural town, you see, do you like racing?
I've got a tip for tomorrow's three-fifteen race: Cara Pálida, five-
to-one, not bad, eh?'

Walking up the steps of the hospital's main entrance, he
thought of the tip: Pale Face, five-to-one. He imagined Bob Hope,
dressed up as a Red Indian, racing around the Hipódromo. Jane
Russell, in black net stockings, was the jockey. How long was
it since he saw that film? Those afternoons spent at El Coliseo
Palermo, El Rosedal, the Cine Park of the calle Thames. El Gran
Norte in front of the little Plaza Malabia.

His father's room was at the end of a long corridor, on the
second floor. He was alone, lying in a bed in a room that was
too big and too empty. Daniel took the only chair, metallic
and lugubrious, and moved it closer to the bed. Everything
was painted an anaemic pink: walls, doors, windows, even

the bed. A small bunch of flowers stood in a jar, which in a previous existence had contained *dulce de leche.*

His father was asleep, but as soon as Daniel sat down he opened his beautiful clear eyes; they were translucent, sky blue, and seemed to radiate a gentle light in the poorly lit room. His father gave a little cry. "You made it just in time, you know, I'd been waiting for you, I'm going to die."Shivers went down Daniel's spine. He put his hand over his father's and silently cried.

"We had some good times together, didn't we?"

"We had some *very* good times together, *papá*, I always had a great time with you."

"When did you come back?'

"Yesterday."

"I'm sorry."

"Don't be silly, *papi*, why are you apologising?'

They remained in silence for a minute, during which time his father kept his eyes closed. Then, he opened them to ask, "Are you OK?'

"I'm well, don't worry."

"No, I don't worry. What happened to your teeth?'

Inevitable. Daniel needed to get to a dentist soon, everybody would be asking the same question. Daniel decided to tell his father the truth; he knew that it would be an acceptable explanation for him.

"They were broken in a fist fight."Not quite a fight; after all, Daniel hadn't had much of a chance to throw any punches.

"Some fists!"said his father.

"He had a knuckleduster, it wasn't a fair contest. What about you? Are you comfortable?'

"I'm OK."His face showed both pain and anguish. He was propped up on two or three big pillows; he had a clear plastic tube sticking up one of his nostrils; another one, secured by white surgical tape, led to a needle inserted in his left arm. Coloured wires were fixed to his chest, monitoring his heartbeat.

"*Mamá* told me that you have a girlfriend in Brazil."Daniel's mother didn't know about Wanda, who would have told her about it? Did she make it up? Or was he inventing it all? "Would you like to bring her over here?"his father asked, knowing it was an absurd idea. First, the apologies; now, a bit of bravado.

"We have other things to worry about right now, the main thing is for you to get better."

At first, his father smiled faintly; then, tears rolled down his cheeks. Daniel took his father's hands between his: they were warm, as usual. He could recall the physical feeling of being afraid as a child – the only thing that saved him was the strong, warm hand of his father.

"Do you think you can get me *Di Yidishe Tsaytung*?"

"What do you want that for?"said Daniel. "You don't read Yiddish."

"My father did."Daniel felt an intense impulse to embrace him. "Besides, the editorials are always in Spanish."

Daniel wondered what could possibly be going through his father's head. "There's a newsagent round the corner; later, I'll see if I can get it,"Daniel said. There was little hope; not many Jews lived in Río Cuarto.

"You should have known my father, he was a good man."

"Everybody in the family always said he was a very special man."

"Did I ever tell you that he made his own wine? He had a big open barrel in the back patio; every year, he bought a mountain of grapes, which were delivered to the house on a dirty old cart. He and a friend would crush them; they rolled up their trousers and danced barefoot in the barrel, laughing while they told stories from the old country."

"No, you've never told me that, were you very close?'

"Not the way you and I have been. He was very strict, he didn't like the things I liked, didn't understand the tango, he didn't smoke, and … he hated soccer."

When Daniel was a child, his father had taken him every other Sunday afternoon to see Boca Juniors at La Bombonera. The day began with a match at 11am – the under-21s. Then, lunch with steak sandwiches. At 1 pm they would watch the reserves, followed by Coca-Cola and ham and cheese sandwiches. Finally, after the sun started to disappear over one side of the stadium, it would be the turn of the first division: Musimessi, *el negro* Colman, *el inglés* Edwards. Lombardo, Mouriño and *el pelado* Pescia. Pierino Gamba, Baiocco, Ferraro, Campana and Busico. What a bunch! El Riachuelo was a party: *Sí, sí, señores, yo soy de Boca/ sí, sí, señores, de corazón/ porque este año, desde la Boca,/ desde la Boca, salió el nuevo campeón.* At the end of the day, *pizza con fainá.* La Bombonera was his second home. On Saturdays, they would sometimes go to a second division match to support Atlanta, in La Paternal –the home for many Jewish *porteños.* Then, on Wednesday evenings, the most *goyishe* activity in the world -to watch amateur boxing at the Luna Park. He remembered, without knowing why, the name of a boxer: Cucuzza Bruno. Daniel had felt immensely privileged. There was never much money, but his father always scraped up enough for football. None of his friends were taken to the matches. But then, one day, his father had an accident. While travelling in a tram, a truck going the wrong way hit the vehicle. In the hospital, he cried and howled and begged the surgeon not to cut off his arm. After two years of repeated surgery, they managed to reconstruct his right arm using pieces of bone taken from his legs and hips. Those were hard days for the family, Daniel had to start working. A friend of the family who owned a successful printing business offered him a job, though it was illegal to employ youngsters below the age of fourteen.

He loved his father, but the accident changed their relationship. Daniel hated having to visit him at the hospital, having to look after him, emptying his bedpan on those hot, humid afternoons, sleeping next to him on the dirty floor. Just when his father most needed his compassion and love, Daniel surprised himself by despising him. His visits to the hospital became shorter and shorter.

Once his father was back home, he spent the long hours of convalescence watching television – a special purchase made by Daniel's mother on credit. It was difficult to believe he would ever recover. Eventually, Daniel left home to share a room in a *pensión*. In the meantime he had changed jobs from the printers to a bank, then to a solicitors' firm. He also did market research on the streets, posted bills at night, and sold dubious plots of land on godforsaken Uruguayan beaches. His father fought his way back to health and returned to work restoring second-hand pianos, earning just enough to pay for rent and groceries. Daniel slowly regained respect for him. He understood the humiliation he had endured. They grew closer again, but they never went back to the Riachuelo together. Never again *pizza con fainá*.

"I took my old man to a soccer match once,"his father recalled. "I finally convinced him after many months of refusing the invitation; it was Boca vs. Lanús. It turned into the most vicious, violent riot, with mounted police and gunfights, a few people died and there were many wounded."He wanted to laugh, but he was crying instead. Soon after, he fell asleep.

When he woke up, he said: "The potatoes are burning, you have to be very careful. Did you hear what happened to your friend Damián? Was he really a Communist?'

"Of course, you know he was. I rang his mother last night. The bastards had been following him. Damián saw it coming. He was planning to leave the country, you know. Many other party leaders had already been taken. I know one thing for sure: Damián wasn't involved in any form of subversion or terrorism. Can you imagine a member of the CP as a *guerrillero*? He was a good militant, very active in the union, an idealist, that's all, *viejo*. He should have been a *guerrillero*, his death would have made more sense."

His father had fallen asleep again. He didn't stay awake for long; either he was very tired, or sedated.

"It's a shame we weren't conquered by the British, isn't it?"He said the next time he woke up.

"Don't say that; they'll think you're a Bolshevik, *un vende-patria.*"

"Imagine: if we had been conquered by the English, we could be like the USA now; not bad, eh? Everyone hates the Yanks, but we all want to be like them; we envy them; if we spoke English today, we wouldn't have these fascist gorillas governing us."

Silence again. The conversation happened in quick bursts, fragments interrupted by short intervals of sleep. Daniel thought of Damián's cousin selling croissants to the exiled Latin American community in Sydney. If the British had conquered Argentina … He knew nothing about Australia – except that eucalyptus, boomerangs and kangaroos came from there. Damián should have accepted his cousin's invitation to join him at the bakery. Better to be covered in flour than dirt.

"I have to ask you for something."

"What? Tell me."

"I don't want to be buried in La Tablada, it's too expensive."

"You're not going to die, *papá.*"

Again, his father started to cry feebly. "I can't go on, I want to give up."

"You're only fifty-two years old, you're still very young."

"My father died when he was fifty, and I always said I would die at the same age, I've already had a few extra years."

"It would be unfair if you disappeared just now, you haven't had any grandchildren yet."

"Things haven't worked out the way I wanted."

"That's not enough reason to hang up the gloves; no point in feeling sorry for yourself."

"I've been so, so unhappy, so miserable."Daniel didn't know what to say; he believed him. "I want to be buried in La Chacarita."

"Next to Gardel?'

Now he gave his son a big smile.

"Promise me."

"I promise you."

If his father felt so strongly about not being buried in a Jewish cemetery, why the request for the Yiddish paper? He knew that he had always felt very Jewish, despite his wish, at times, to hide it. Daniel well knew how much his father had suffered from the anti-Semitism in the neighbourhood where he grew up. Every match he played for the Maccabbi Football Club used to end in a fight: "They always expected us to come out to play wearing *peyess.*"His father was feeling guilty for never having made any money. He didn't want his family to spend what they didn't have on his funeral. Maybe he was feeling ashamed as well. Daniel remembered the monthly visits by the Chevra Kaddisha, which administered the cemetery. Everybody knew that they inflated the prices, according to the family's income. They were right not to trust people: some rich Jews tried hard to hide their fortunes from them. But if one hadn't contributed enough during life, one would end up dead in a Gentile cemetery. Worse than going to Hell.

"Could you cut my toenails? I hate having them so long."Such an intimate request. "The nurse also said I needed a haircut."

So far, no nurse had shown up; nobody had come to see whether he was OK or if he needed anything. He proceeded to cut his father's toenails with his little pocket-knife scissors.

"Is *el papagayo* around?"Daniel almost fell off his chair: first, he asked about Wanda –without knowing anything about her. Now, he was asking about Joacaría. "It should be under the bed,"his father added.

It took him a few seconds to realise that he was referring to the bottle that patients used to urinate in; it was called *el papagayo* in Buenos Aires. He didn't find it under the bed but in the little metal bedside cupboard. He drew back the sheets, trying not to disturb the wires on his chest. Why did his father seem to be in so much pain? He was going to call a nurse and ask her about it. Was there anything else that could be done for him? The trousers of his father's pyjamas were unbuttoned; Daniel placed his father's penis inside the *papagayo*. It was a long piss. Afterwards, Daniel took the container to the sink at the other side of the room, and rinsed it out.

"The hospital chaplain came around yesterday; he asked whether I wanted to make a confession."

"What did you say?'

""I'm a Jew," I told him. "You mean an Israelite," *el boludo*, the poor *schlemiel* corrected me. They think the word *Jew* is an insult. I said: "No! I'm no Israelite, nor am I Israeli. One hundred per cent Jewish!" I explained. I didn't want any forgiveness, either from his God or mine. I'm a Jew of the Diaspora, and as such, God should ask *me* for forgiveness, *He* is the one who's sinned against us."

His father seemed convinced he was going to die, it was unbearable.

"Did you fly from Buenos Aires? How was it?'

"OK. The plane was half empty ... You've never flown in an aeroplane, have you?"

"No."

"How come?'

"I don't know."

Daniel couldn't understand why his father had never learned to swim, or ever tried to drive a car. It hadn't been just poverty.

He had fallen asleep again; this time, more deeply than before. Daniel needed a toilet; his search for one took him to the other side of the ward. On his way back, he came across a nurse in the corridor; she looked confident and busy. He introduced himself, and before he could say anything else, she declared: "You father will be OK, don't worry about it, everything is under control, the doctor saw him before you came and checked him. If you need anything, just press the bell above his bed."And off she went.

Upon his return, he was still asleep; Daniel sat on the chair. What would happen if his father were to die? He would have to take care of his mother and sisters; he would have to work, stop fucking around with his desire to be a poet. He would have to prove to the world that he could be a grown-up. No one earned a living writing poetry, or even writing novels. Not in Argentina, anyway. A lot of his friends were turning to journalism; he knew that he would find it impossible to do that.

He was lost in thought when his father woke up with a horrible cough, choking, gasping for air. He jerked forward and tried to say something, but no words came; his tongue was pushed out with every cough, as if he was going to throw up; blood rushed to his head. Daniel immediately pressed the bell, and shouted for help. His father went on coughing, not getting enough air. Leaning forward in one of his spasms, he pulled the oxygen tube out of his nose. Daniel was struggling to put it back in when the two nurses arrived. Behind them, a young doctor came running. Daniel moved away from the bed, stepped back toward the door, and stood just outside the room, not able to see what they were doing to his father. "He's really going to die,"he thought. And then, "It's not possible, Daddy, don't die, don't even think of it, don't leave me, *carajo.*"

The doctor didn't seem to be doing anything at all; he gave instructions to the nurses, who fluttered nervously around him. One of them hurried out to get something and said to Daniel, "Why don't you sit in the waiting room? You'll be more comfortable?'

As if comfort was what counted.

He found a chair in the corridor, put it near the door, and sat down. He felt cold. Time didn't seem to pass. There was complete silence now, Daniel could hear his own breathing. Then he saw the nurse come back with a syringe and some ampoules. Finally, the doctor came through the door. How much time had passed? He turned to Daniel and solemnly said: "I'm sorry, I'm afraid we couldn't do anything to save him. Your father has passed away."

He rang his mother and sisters. While the nurses took his father's body away, Daniel put the few clothes he found in the metal cupboard in the room in a plastic bag, and the leftover medicines in another. The nurses made it clear that since they had already been included in the bill, they belonged to his family. He didn't know why they would want those pills, tablets, capsules, drops and injections, and four ampoules of morphine.

Daniel struck a deal with the administration of the clinic. They would allow him to remove his father's body so it could be taken to Buenos Aires straight away in an ambulance; the death certificate would only be released by the driver against payment of the hospital bill, plus the money owed to the funeral directors for the coffin and transport. Daniel's mother proved once again her ability to deal with difficult situations; she was always surprising him. After having expressed her concern about the finances of it all on the phone to Daniel, she had approached uncle Gershon. He wasn't rich but he had a generous heart; he was married to one of his father's sisters, and had always helped anybody in the family who had been in financial need. In principle, he agreed to pay for the lot, but expected to be paid back in small monthly instalments. Daniel was very grateful to his uncle Gershon for the offer.

It was ten in the evening when Daniel finally made it to the funeral parlour. Choosing the coffin was a farce. The undertaker had probably been ready to go to sleep when he received the telephone call from the hospital; he was trying his best to be polite. Daniel was invited to choose from dozens of different coffins, neatly displayed on big shelves in a storage room behind a small chapel, all of them open and waiting to be occupied by people that were no more. The man explained the characteristics and benefits of different kinds of wood, the quality of the lining, the intricate trimmings and decorations that would accompany his father on his long journey home. When Daniel finally decided on the cheapest -a standard, plain coffin- the man couldn't hide his disappointment: "Well, the important thing,"the undertaker said, "is that Our Lord will welcome his soul; his body will rest in *this* in the cemetery."

Daniel still had to go to the hotel where his father had stayed and collect whatever he had left behind.

It was a small hotel situated near the river that divided the town. The room had been paid for in advance by his father's friend Juan Carlos, who had travelled with him and was now back in Buenos Aires. The owner, a fat and loud woman, wore a dress that looked like a Bedouin tent and smoked a pipe held tightly between her teeth; she opened her mouth only to swear and spit with real gusto into a white container by her chair. One of the walls in the hotel lobby was dominated by a big sign: *Se Prohibe Escupir en el Suelo* – it is forbidden to spit on the floor. She led him to the room and started chatting away:

"Do you believe that our souls are immortal, or do you think that when one dies, that's it! The end of all ends?"The woman didn't wait for an answer. It was hard to believe, but like many other rooms that Daniel had seen in *pensiones*, it had no windows. With no fresh air or ventilation, the place was musty; years of cigarette smoke had impregnated the flowery wallpaper. A bare bulb, hanging from the centre of the ceiling, shone a useless yellowish light. The bed had been left unmade and the door of the wardrobe hung half-open.

Daniel took all the clothes out and put them on the bed. Leaning against the door-frame, she continued: "I just hope that there is Hell and that my husband spends eternity there. He was the cruellest man that ever lived; he refused to give it to me for the last twenty years of his life and then died fucking a young whore in a brothel in Córdoba. He had a heart attack, just like your father, except that my husband died straight away;

he kicked the bucket while screwing, the sonofabitch. Not a bad way to go."

Daniel looked at her; he was angry, not necessarily at her.

"If you need me, I'll be downstairs,"she said, and disappeared.

Daniel found a suitcase in a corner and packed everything in it: two pairs of trousers, three dirty shirts, a couple of ties, underwear, socks, an old pair of black rubber galoshes. As he packed mechanically, he thought about his father, he remembered Damián. "At least I am a son burying his father, not the other way round."He couldn't get away from thinking of Damián's mother, of the circumstances of her son's death. Laura and the children had left the country; they were already in Spain. Now Damián's mother, widowed long ago, was moving from one friend's house to another; she couldn't bear to be alone, she was afraid of going mad.

Carrying the suitcase from the hotel to the clinic under the starry sky, Daniel thought of the first lines of the National Anthem, which the police had played loudly to hide Damián's cries:

> *Listen, mortals, the sacred cry:*
> *Freedom! Freedom! Freedom!*

Daniel was told that la Ruta 8 wasn't too bad. *"Si Dios quiere* – God willing,"said the undertaker, "it should take you about seven hours."He was lying: the road was full of potholes, and even with God's help, it was impossible to reach Buenos Aires in less than nine hours.

Profundo Mariscal, the driver, looked like a direct descendant of the Comechingones. He had features transmitted from one generation to the next by eternal genes: thick black hair, slanted eyes, dark olive skin, the flattened nose of a boxer – the only traces of the indigenous culture that survived the Conquest. While systematically murdering the Indians, the Spaniards had also conquered the Americas by fornicating their women.

Profundo's features conveyed tranquillity. Dressed in a wrinkled jacket and a mismatched tie, the man had brought along a thermos full of coffee and a brown paper bag with enough pastries to feed a soccer team. They departed close to midnight: Profundo at the wheel; Daniel in the passenger seat; his father, lying peacefully and eternally silent, in the back.

A line from *Hamlet* came to mind: "*... all that live must die...* "Well, who could argue with that? Certainly not those already dead like his father, nailed as he was into his coffin. For him, to die had been an act of freedom; his final gesture, his last wish. On one of those long nights in Rio, when they used to talk until the early hours of the morning, Olinda declared that the only thing she wanted was to leave a mark in the world – not a child, like David, but something for which she could be remembered after her death. She really couldn't complain, she already had her paintings hung in the Museu de Arte Moderna. What had his father left? And what Eugenio? And Damián? He was certain of one thing: what a waste, not to have been able to spend more time together!

"Would you like *una factura, señor?*"Profundo asked him. "What about some coffee?'

Daniel refused both. Nothing could compare with those little sweet *carioca* coffees; they weren't the only thing that he missed from Brazil. Earlier that day, he had been composing a letter in his mind to Wanda. He had a lot to tell her.

He pondered the explanations that the doctor at the hospital had given him: his father had suffered from chronic bronchitis, which had caused his heart to fail. "Too much pressure in the pulmonary arteries,"the doctor had said. Forty cigarettes a day hadn't helped. Mornings at home had always been marked by his father's coughing. "It's just a normal smoker's cough, there's nothing to it,"his father would say to anyone who cared to ask him about it.

What had he been thinking before? Ah, yes, leaving a mark in the world ... He was troubled by the future, how was he going to support his mother and sisters? It was all very well to feel that now he had to be a grown-up, but how was he going to manage? Was he a real writer? And if he was, what was he going to do? He felt mildly envious of Olinda, thinking unreasonably, "It's easier for painters". He knew this wasn't true. How did it start, this involvement with literature? The incident with *Señorita* Calvo didn't explain it all. How was he going to prove that he was a writer, a poet, if not by writing?

Daniel suddenly opened his eyes and looked at Profundo. Something had happened, how long had they been on the road? The driver had been nodding, was he falling asleep? Maybe it hadn't been tranquillity and peace of mind that he conveyed on his face: he had been falling asleep from the very start!

"Are you OK?" he dared to ask.

"I'm fine, *señor*," the man said.

"Would you like some coffee?" Daniel now offered. He was worried: he was sure the driver was falling asleep. Great. Fantastic. Terrific. Profundo accepted the offer: "Only half a cup." His manner clearly said: "Leave me alone."

Daniel helped Profundo first, then served himself a full cup. He wished he had some brandy to go with it, something to make him feel brave. As long as Profundo was holding the cup, he knew the man was awake. He didn't want to die while taking his father to the funeral in an ambulance.

He wasn't given much time to think any further. Profundo Mariscal was dreaming of faraway places when he completely missed a bend. The ambulance went straight ahead, flying from the tarmac over the side of the road and down a steep bank. The vehicle did a complete turn and landed on its wheels, rolling on for another fifty meters. It came to a halt at the edge of a pool formed by recent torrential rain. Everything happened so fast, Daniel thought he was watching a movie: images of cars blowing up filled his head, but the engine wasn't producing any smoke, and everything seemed so silent, so quiet. They both got out of the ambulance as quickly as they could.

Was he alive?

Profundo was standing in front of the vehicle, his face illuminated by the headlights, which were still on. Daniel became enraged, maddened by the man's colossal recklessness. He ran up to the driver: "*Hijo de puta,* you motherfucker, how can you fall asleep like that? I knew it, Goddammit, I knew it! *Pelotudo de mierda,* you fucker…"

The man must have thought Daniel was going to kill him: "I'm sorry, I couldn't refuse the job, we're desperate, I have a child who's ill."

Daniel was ready to hit Profundo but suddenly stopped. At one moment, he could really have murdered him; a second later, he was feeling sorry. "You fucking asshole, that's no reason to kill both of us," he finally said. And looking towards the back of the ambulance, where his father was, he added, "Besides…"But he couldn't finish.

Then the lights of the ambulance went out.

The temperature had dropped. El Pampero blew the cold from Patagonia across the plains, all the way to the cotton plantations and the red *quebracho* forests of the Chaco province. That wind was capable of affecting people's moods: young lovers made death pacts and lonely people hanged themselves in the middle of the night.

Profundo Mariscal had gone to get help. There was a petrol station further up the road, which was supposed to be open all night. Profundo reassured him that he knew the place well, they were close to the province of Santa Fé. Profundo was going to call his boss and ask him to send another vehicle. "I don't give a damn about another ambulance, just ask him for another driver,"Daniel remarked. They couldn't afford another calamity.

Daniel didn't trust him, but there, in the middle of the Pampas, he didn't have too many options. He watched Profundo disappear into the night. The powerful lights of heavy trucks occasionally illuminated Ruta 8. Looking around warily as if somebody could possibly be there, Daniel pulled down his trousers and squatted by the side of the ambulance. With his back exposed to the wind, unable to see anything, he prayed that there were no *tarántulas* or *yararás* around. But Daniel was aware that in spite of his efforts to be rational and composed, he couldn't help jumping every time the tall grass brushed against his skin.

In the dark, squatting by the now useless vehicle, he tried to imagine the countryside around him. The monotony of the pampas had always fascinated him. On those huge plains that went on forever, trees had long since been replaced by grass to feed the cattle of the *estancias*. From where he was, Daniel could make out the shape of an *ombú*, a tree that wasn't even a proper tree but a gigantic herbaceous excrescence, a vegetable monster that gave plenty of shade but couldn't be used as firewood. In one of its branches he could just make out the nest of an *hornero*.

Cold and miserable, he declared, "I shit on you, bloody oligarchs."

He wiped himself with bits torn from a newspaper found at the front of the ambulance. This had been the method normally used in his house. They had a bidet, everybody did in Buenos Aires, but they used the previous day's *Clarín*, always at hand in a corner of the bathroom –no money for fancy toilet paper. He smiled at the idea of getting to destination with the weather forecast printed on his ass.

He cleaned his hands by rubbing them on the damp grass. Then, he tried to open the back door of the ambulance, but the impact had badly twisted it. "You might have to be buried ambulance and all, *viejo.*"He moved to the front, climbed into the seat and forced his way through the small windows with white curtains that divided the front from the rear. The back compartment was stuffy: what had possessed him to get in there? The coffin seemed secure enough, there was nothing to check.

Daniel immediately felt oppressed. Without taking his eyes off the coffin, he sat on the floor of the ambulance; gradually, he was overcome by grief; he sobbed and wailed and called out to his father. *"Papito, mi papito…"* Soon, his sadness turned into anger, a mad rage that made him first kick and then hit the coffin with his hands while screaming at the top of his voice "Why? Why did you die, *hijo de puta* – son of a bitch? Why did you leave us? *Idiota! Carajo!* Why the hell did you have to go like this, so unhappy?"

And to his complete surprise an unexpected demand came from his throat, "And why did you have to sell my sole possession, the only thing I truly loved, my typewriter? Why didn't you tell me that you were in such a bad way, that you didn't have a penny? Why did you lie to me?'

Daniel couldn't keep the promise he had made to his father. "If he is buried in La Chacarita," Uncle Gershon had said, "don't count on me, I'm not paying." And in his blunt, candid way, he asked, "Am I going to pay for one of ours to be buried with the *goyim*? He was my brother-in-law, it's a *Miztvah* for me, you understand? His soul must rest in peace in a Jewish cemetery; if not, he'll come back to haunt us all."

Daniel found it difficult to accept, but secretly he was relieved. What was the alternative, anyway? Uncle Gershon paid the money owed to the driver who had replaced Profundo Mariscal at the wheel of the new ambulance. He thanked his uncle; they embraced in front of all the relatives who had been waiting for the ambulance outside his mother's house.

If they were rich, dead Jews didn't have to travel far from the city, they were taken to the cemetery in Liniers; if they were poor, the trip was the long one to Berazatégui. It would remain a mystery how Daniel's mother had managed to get a space for his father at La Tablada –another expensive cemetery. She must have saved for years, penny by penny, setting aside the change from the daily housekeeping.

At the cemetery, they had to wait for the purification of the body, the *taharah*, which was performed by three members of the Chevra Kadisha. They washed the body thoroughly with warm water, from head to foot, including all the orifices. Years ago, one of his older cousins had invented horrific stories about the *taharah*. Daniel knew now that there was no question of putting a hose up the arse of a dead man.

"Did you take the wedding-ring off his finger?"enquired Aunt Paula. Daniel said he hadn't. "That was stupid, now it'll get stolen, do you think *they* bury the dead with their gold?'

Wanda, *filha do São Salvador do Bonfim*, where are you?

From a distance, Rabbi Tapolsky called Daniel and beckoned for him to come closer. "May the Omnipresent comfort you along with the rest of the mourners of Zion and Jerusalem."He didn't know how to respond, so he said nothing. What should one say in those circumstances? Then the Rabbi turned around and asked him to follow. In a room in a building at the entrance of the cemetery, his dead father's body was lying in the casket, under the shroud, ready for burial; his face was covered; a *shomer* kept watch next to him.

"I included a *tallis* in the coffin, even a non-observant Jew should have one when he departs from this world. Otherwise,"the Rabbi explained, "when the resurrection takes place, he'll look like a *schlemiel*, God forbid, not having a *tallis* to perform God's commandments."

"I'm grateful to you, Rebbe."

The Rabbi asked him to open his right hand and then poured some dust in it. At this point, the *shomer* uncovered his father's face. The Rabbi said, "you should scatter this, which comes from the Mount of Olives, over your father's eyes. It's an act of filial respect. "From dust we come and to dust we return ...'"

Daniel did as he was told. Immediately afterwards, two other men came in and covered the coffin. Then the Rabbi invited him to perform the *keriah* – the rending of the garments, symbol of a torn and broken heart. Daniel wasn't prepared for this: first, he cut into the lapel of his jacket with a little pair of scissors offered by the *shomer*; then, he tore open the cut. Daniel realised – perhaps for the first time – the enormity of his loss. He felt no consolation: his father was gone. Forever. Nothing could change his own destiny, his father's life was already part of the past. He cried in desperation and silently. This time, without anger.

He was given time to regain his calm and then the casket was wheeled out by the men. Outside, Daniel joined his mother and sisters, who also had to perform *keriah*. His mother couldn't quite handle it, she collapsed into tears. Miriam, who was only twelve, kept biting her lower lip in a repetitive manner; she also finally broke down. Shoshana, three years older, appeared dignified and confident, but Daniel could see the terror in her eyes. They all embraced.

The procession stopped several times on the way to the grave. After the funeral, Rabbi Tapolsky explained the tradition: each stop represented a stage of life. A one-year-old was like a king, loved by everybody, indulged by all. After that, the child was considered to be like a pig wallowing in the mud. By ten, boys were like he-goats, oblivious to the damage they might be causing. By twenty, he had become a stallion, grooming himself, searching for a mate. After marriage, the poor man resembled a donkey carrying a heavy load, burdened with the responsibility of a wife. When the children arrived, he was compared to a courageous dog, desperately striving to support his family. Daniel's father was spared the last stage, that of old age; he would have become senile and ridiculous, like a monkey.

Every time the procession stopped, Daniel could hear his Uncle Gershon, talking with Uncle Jaime – his voice in competition with the *chazzen* reciting the Psalms. His lament was of this world: how the *schwartzers* were invading the city, making it violent and dirty; how Perón was to blame; he had been a false Messiah, and now, years later, everybody was having to pay for his mistakes;

how the military were punishing the Jews for crimes they had
never committed; the exchange rate for the dollar on the day. At
first, Daniel had felt like turning around and shouting at them to
shut up, but, after all, life had to go on, why not?

The coffin was slowly lowered into the grave. The Rabbi gave
the spade to Daniel: "Three spadefuls,"he commanded, "one for
the soul, one for the spirit, one for the breath."After he completed
the task, he passed the shovel to his mother, who in turn gave it
to each of his sisters. Everyone present took a turn; the grave was
filled. Meanwhile, the *chazzen* never stopped singing beautiful,
soulful, supplicating prayers. Daniel felt transported, part of a
tradition that he couldn't understand.

Aunt Paula had been in charge of negotiating with the *chazzen*.
Most of them stood at the entrance to the cemetery, waiting for
customers. She had chosen a tall, handsome man with a jet-black
beard, wearing a long, elegant coat; he looked like an actor. The
cantor's fees were determined by how long they sang. For the
first time in her life, Aunt Paula didn't haggle. Later, while the
chazzen was performing his duty, her eyes betrayed a pleasure
that God wouldn't have sanctioned in those circumstances.

The *Tzidduk Ha-Din* was recited: "The Lord has given and the
Lord has taken away ...'

Before leaving the cemetery, the Rabbi asked everybody to
wash their hands. Then he said to Daniel, "Remember, no leather
shoes, no shaving, no haircuts, no gel on your hair, and above
all,"the Rabbi looked intently into Daniel's eyes, "no sex for
seven days'.

Wanda, please come and sing *Antonico* for me.

Play a samba.

Be sweet to me, *O Bahiana*.

2

Heavy rains brought chaos to Buenos Aires: streets flooded, bus drivers became frantic and taxi drivers went mad. It was dangerous to walk on the streets: one could be mercilessly soaked by the passing cars, stumble on loose cobblestones, or slip in the mud. Worse still, one could simply fall into one of the many ditches that labourers left uncovered for months. In the evening, once the rain stopped, the city transformed itself. A special atmosphere enveloped the cafés and bars in Calle Corrientes. People spent hours gathered around the tables of La Comedia and La Paz, the windows open to let the cool air blow in from the river after the storm. They talked about literature and films, soccer and pornography, theatre and politics. The Paris of the Americas. In that city, there was an optimism that even the *mufa porteña* had not yet managed to defeat.

Luigi and Daniel had arranged to meet at one of their favourite restaurants, in calle Paraná. Before their trip to Brazil, on the first Friday of every month, they used to celebrate payday by going out to a restaurant. To eat well, to be served by a waiter, to be able to pay the bill, even to leave a tip, was a silly ceremony, but it restored their hopes that they were like the rest of the world, that they could also make a living. They would eat nothing all day until they met at the restaurant. They studied the menu (which they knew by heart), settling on the same order every time: ravioli with pesto and tomato sauce, T-bone steak with a little salt and lots of *chimichurri*, mixed salad with onions, and for dessert, a piece of fresh Provolone with *membrillo* -quince jelly. All this accompanied by two litres of red wine. Easily, two litres.

On the phone, while arranging to meet, Daniel noticed that Luigi didn't sound too happy. Daniel asked himself, "I wonder if his mother is ill". But Luigi's only comment was, "I've got lots to tell you."

Luigi was already at the table when Daniel arrived. They shook hands and then embraced.

"How was it?"Luigi would have wanted to get back to Buenos Aires for the funeral, but in the end he had stayed with his mother and Joacaría in Sierra de la Ventana.

"It wasn't exactly a carnival."

The waiter, an old Hungarian émigré who had mysteriously managed to escape from his country after the 1956 uprising, interrupted them, "*Muchachos*, I don't know why you insist on coming to this joint."

"We love you, Teodor, that's the only reason,"Luigi joked.

Teodor looked his usual dejected self. Leaning over the table, he whispered: "The rats are taking over the kitchen, we're losing the war against them."

"It happens everywhere, Magyar, out there, the rats are winning too."

"I'm not talking about politics, I'm not interested in that shit. I'm serious. Don't you believe me? The boss called in a company that specialises in killing vermin; the beasts are really big and very fast. They come across from the empty theatre at the back, behind the kitchen … Anyway, they filled the place with poison, they said it was foolproof, guaranteed for a year. So, what happened? Our two cats, our only hope in this Godforsaken place, ate the rat poison and died. Stupid animals! What can I say? I think they decided to commit suicide. It's an unjust world, I tell you ... So, what would you like to eat today?'

Teodor was a great asset to the restaurant trade.

They ordered. "And bring some soda and ice for the wine!"shouted Daniel as the waiter walked away. "I'm thirsty."

"Me too,"added Luigi.

"I've heard from Olinda ,"Luigi said.

"How is she?'

"She's OK, she sends her love. Apparently, the reunion with her son was marvellous; she sounded really happy. But listen to this: it seems that our friend Socrates, the mean-spirited spiritualist, has turned into a popular hero. Olinda claims that he's the political leader of the transvestites, he is running for election."

"You're kidding me."

"I swear it."

"Well, anything can happen in that country. Do you miss it?'

"What, Brazil? Very much."The restaurant filled up with the crowds emerging from the movies and the theatres; the noise had risen sharply.

"I have something much more important to tell you,"Luigi sounded gloomy. "Joacaría died."

"*Merda*! How?'

"It's ironic, the vet said that his heart just gave out."

"I didn't know animals could have heart attacks."

"It wasn't a heart attack, he died of sorrow. He wasn't ever himself again, he was never happy at my mother's house. I guess he knew I was planning to leave him there for a while. Now I feel terribly guilty for having brought him, I shouldn't have."

The parrot had been a good friend.

"You loved him too much to leave him behind."

"Yes, but it's pretty clear he should have stayed in Rio. It was cruel to smuggle him. I was thinking only of myself. He would have been happy living with Olinda and her son by the banks of the Sâo Francisco."Luigi was feeling true remorse, the mortification experienced by a mourner for a loved one. But there was more to come.

"Listen, I can't go back to Brazil. I'm staying here – well, not even in Buenos Aires, I'm leaving for Bariloche in a couple of days. A friend of mine has a bar there and offered me a job as a barman. At least I can get away from this madhouse. The money isn't much, but the guy told me, "You'll be able to get more girls than Gardel and Frank Sinatra together."'

Absurd. Surely, that wasn't the reason for Luigi to go. He could understand his decision not to return to Brazil but he was deeply saddened by it, realising that he would feel lonely. In Buenos Aires, the repression had begun to be felt more acutely. The South wasn't a bad place, except for the rumours that, every year, a group of Nazis and their descendants still celebrated Hitler's birthday over there. Daniel wondered what he was going to do. He had no doubts, he had to stay in Buenos Aires, at least for a while. He was now responsible for his mother and his sisters, who would feel lost without him.

"I'm going to miss you."

"Me too."

"I wrote a poem for my father,"Daniel said after a while. "I brought it with me."

"Go ahead, read it."

Depending on their mood, they would read their poems and short stories to each other in bars and restaurants. At the beginning of their friendship, they used to feel a bit embarrassed and inhibited by other people, but they soon overcame that. So what, if others heard them? The more, the better.

Daniel read:

... I was the last to see him in that room with the gloomy doorway
in that clinic in the centre of town

in that city full of schoolgirls and lady piano teachers.
How am I going to forget the joy in your eyes
that looked just like mine?
How am I going to forget
that oxygen cylinder and the rubber tube insolently up your nose?
How am I going to forget the cry
that you imposed on your tortured heart
the strong hug that you gave me
the caresses that your legs
your arms your back demanded from me
drying your forehead holding your hand?
How am I going to forget your cursed confession
your last wish that I couldn't fulfil
the disquiet that you suffered?
Now
just one step from your death
a long second from dying
you couldn't ignore anything any more
you couldn't hide anything
the unhappiness of your life
the uselessness of life
the true colours of life.

You have died and other fathers like you
and other sons like me will follow us.
I will take your place
and your unknown grandchildren will take mine.
You have died and injustice will continue in the world
and war will continue in the world.
You have died for nothing.
You have died and I'll go on by the window
waiting for some torrential rain
wondering if with your suicide you attain real peace
if this is the only way to live and communicate.

You have died
and I will continue to wonder
about my uncertain future
about my desire to be a drifter
a pirate a popular singer.
I will continue wondering
because I have no desire to be anything special
because I fervently refuse to grow up
or because my way of growing up is different
from all other known ways of growing up.

After he had finished reading, the two of them remained silent. Then, Luigi said, "I want you to give me a copy."

Daniel looked at the clock on the opposite wall: it was half past two in the morning. They called Teodor. They wanted more wine.

Soon afterwards, Luigi left for the South.

The death of his dearly beloved bird had deeply affected him. It represented the end of an era: his love affair with Olinda and with Brazil was over. Daniel accompanied Luigi to Plaza Constitución, where his friend took the train to Bariloche. That morning, he received a postcard from Wanda: "I have offered you a strength much greater than myself and I don't know what I demand from you. Love, Wanda". All the passion he had felt for her, the memory of a feeling that he had temporarily forgotten, came back to haunt him with a precision he welcomed. In contrast to Luigi, it was clear to Daniel that he *had* to return to Brazil. How could he not go back to Wanda?

The circumstances of Damián's death had convinced him that the rules of the game had changed. They had always wanted to believe that literature, just as much as politics, was a weapon to combat ignorance, prejudice and the injustice of the world. But politics bored them, and given the repressive government they now lived under, poetry was no longer enough to confront the brutality of the police and the military. As a child, he lived in fear that one day they would come and take his father away – he voted for the Radical Party, most of the neighbours were Peronists. Even Boca Juniors fans became a threat when they started singing for Evita and for Perón. Every so often one heard a story: the caretaker's wife had denounced the grocer for having called Evita a whore; the baker had been tortured because of his son's political activity at the university; a leader of the Socialist Party had been castrated in jail. Daniel remembered the grownups joking about *la picana* –the electric prod, another great Argentinian invention with no patent. The police had been using it since the Thirties – a source of national pride.

Yes, the danger of a *yarará* in the middle of the countryside would have been preferable to the forces of evil and hatred.

Daniel was lucky enough to get a job with the same small company he had worked for previously, doing market research. He hated it. He had to get stupid questionnaires filled on soft drinks, condoms, TV programmes, toothpaste, sewing machines, chocolate-flavoured chewing gum. The money was good: in a few months, he could save enough for a one-way ticket to Brazil. During the day, he moved from one neighbourhood to another locating the people to be interviewed. At night, Daniel went back to sticking up posters for the art galleries. He was determined to leave as soon as possible.

It was already midnight when he found himself standing at the corner of Florida and Paraguay. It smelled like rain. He prepared the paste for the posters. With a wide brush, he mixed the powdered glue with water in a five-litre paint can. His hands were becoming stiff, it was too cold. He was hoping the police wouldn't hassle him, anything could provoke them. Once, Daniel had been reprimanded by two uniformed policemen for kissing Lola just outside la Biblioteca del Maestro. "It's illegal to do this in public, you know that we can book you," they had warned them.

Onganía y la remilputaqueloreparió.

That night's posters were for an exhibition by Carlos Alonso, one of his favourite painters. For a second, he imagined he had been invited to the opening. He could meet all those girls, attractive daughters of the upper classes, stunning women who attended cultural events, wanting to be seduced by successful artists. They would tell him endless stories about their trips to Europe, the prizes at the latest Venice Biennale, the Cannes Film Festival, the opera season in Milan. He knew he was envious of their money, their casual French expressions, their Earl Grey and Lapsang Souchong teas, their malt whiskies and clothes from Harrods. He despised himself for feeling such envy, but he couldn't help it. They had so much money, while he had to bust his ass getting enough money together for one measly ticket to Rio.

He started down Florida, sticking posters in any available space – especially, over other posters. Was he ever going to find a job that suited him? Suddenly, in front of the windows of a fashionable shop, something caught his eye. The bird was standing on a pile of fake gold coins, a faint smile across his face. It was a ridiculous, farcical display: British pirates were bringing the latest yachting wear to the Argentinian shores. Joacaría couldn't have been mistaken for any other parrot. It was him! Daniel could recognise the colour of his plumage, his demeanour – except that they had not only embalmed his body, but in the process they had also replaced his wooden leg with one made of plastic -or maybe wax.

Luigi had told him that the vet in Sierra de la Ventana had asked permission to mummify Joacaría. He convinced him by saying that the parrot was a very special specimen; it was unusual to have access to a *Deropytus accipitrinus accipitrinus*. And the bird had such a human expression on his face! The children from the primary schools in the area would be eternally grateful to Luigi if he agreed to allow his bird to be embalmed. Now there he was, forever preserved, sold to an interior decorator for good money.

It was likely that the primary school children had been left with nothing but a photograph. Even in death, Joacaría looked alive and seemed to be enjoying himself. Daniel could almost imagine hearing him through the glass, shouting, *"Kish me in tochis!'*

He didn't know how long he'd been standing there. When Daniel finally recovered from his astonishment, he looked into the mummified parrot's glass eyes and said, "Delighted to see you again, Joacaría, even in these circumstances."

As he walked away, he shouted, "At least you'll get to see lots of girls go by."

The rain started to pour down on the deserted streets and he said to himself, "some things will never die."

1971

Five years later, in the middle of that extraordinary concert at the Teatro Castro Alves in Bahía, just as Caetano Veloso was finishing *Você Nâo Entende de Nada* and Chico Buarque de Hollanda started on *Cotidiano*, during the prolonged instant when one song became the next and the rhythm imposed by the guitar and the drums was driving the audience crazy and people danced and shouted and then remained in silence, not knowing which way the musicians were going, where they were transporting them, and people danced more and shouted and celebrated, Caetano repeating *"eu quero'*, and Chico *"todo o dia'*, yes, right there and then, Daniel saw him over the multitude of heads jumping up and down. It was Andrés Steinberg, running towards him out of nowhere, shouting "Daniel! Daniel! Shit! *Me cago en dios!* Daniel! I've been looking for you everywhere, in Buenos Aires, in Rio, in Sâo Paulo, man, where were you?"And as he approached, he exclaimed, "I come to find you here! Can you feel the energy in this place? Man, the vibes are so positive, this music, this madness, look at everybody's faces, *hermano*, peace, bro', peace and love."And Daniel didn't really know whether he was that pleased to see Andrés but, anyway, his old friend from the early days in Buenos Aires went on, "I've been to New York, man, fuck! *That* is big like, *really* big, with Big Capital Letters, BIG!"Daniel continued. "It just blew my mind, oh man, everybody is just going crazy over there, dropping acid and everything's really cool, man, far out."And he went on like that while Caetano and Chico started on *Os Argonautas,* and Daniel wanted Andrés to disappear but he had to ask, "What did you want to see me for?"And Andrés said, "You've done well in leaving the country, man, Lanusse and the new Junta don't know their heads from their asses, it's a complete mess, and, yes, I've been looking for you all over the place.""You told me that already.""Yes, right, right, I wanted to let you know that I saw Allen Ginsberg in New York.""And so?""He read the poem for your dead father in the corner of a room in this apartment where I met him."And now the music stopped, the concert was over but people were shouting for "more! More!"And Caetano and Chico reappeared on stage and people went wild. "I had to tell you,"Andrés continued, "Ginsberg read your poem from the copy of your book which Manuel had sent him!""Did he really read it? In Spanish?""Yes! In Spanish, man, I don't know if he understood anything but he read it anyway."And Daniel knew then, beyond any doubt, that *that* piece of news uttered on a tropical November night in the Teatro Castro Alves in Salvador, Bahía, that isolated event, irrelevant to the rest of his life and completely immaterial to the movement of the stars and the tides of the sea, probably made up by Andrés anyway to give himself importance, that single moment marked the end of his youth.

1986

2

*Q*uerido Damián,

    You are dead, and I have survived. Twenty years after your senseless and brutal torture, your pointless murder, your presence in my memory persists – still urgent, for ever insistent. It hasn't been easy for me to acknowledge it but, while living in Rio, I managed to ignore your letters. At the time, that was not difficult. Far away, Luigi and I lived unaware of our destinies. Against all evidence, we kept our hopes alive, we wanted to believe that the future could still belong to us. Afterwards, in the seventies, a truly violent, cruel and repressive earthquake hit the country. So much suffering. Such heartless persecution. Your name was added to a long list of murdered people, of the tortured and desaparecidos. Thirty thousand of them: workers, students, journalists, lawyers, medical doctors. Pregnant young women. Adolescent boys and girls. Grandparents. Some of our best friends. Pablo Klimovsky. Federico Gorbea. Miguel Angel Bustos. Jorge Calvo. Some of them with a number: Rodolfo Jorge Walsh, File No. 2587. Roberto Jorge Santoro, File No. 3832. I have kept one of his books of poems, with his signature: "Daniel, congratulations on your book. *Poetry or death.* Venceremos! *Roberto."But nobody won. I've met your mother a few times around Plaza Italia, hair all white, limping a little, consumed by her inconsolable tragedy. She smiled at me and I kissed her warmly on her cheek. She still asks, por qué? Por qué? Why? What to say? All there's left is this desire that things could have been different, that all those friends should have survived. I wish that you could have been with us, walking in Lapa, ignorant of dangers, discovering that wonderful music, writing these lines.*

Daniel

Acknowledgements

The Comte de Lautréamount wished that poetry should be written by all, not just by one person alone. The present novel has certainly been written by many. Sometimes unwittingly, people contributed with their histories and dreams, their conversations and fantasies. That *Gregorio Kohon* appears as the author of this book is one more triumph of the imagination.

I am immeasurably grateful to several friends, too many to name, who worked very hard on various versions of the manuscript, offering their generous comments and criticisms. I would like to thank two of my editors, who specially contributed in the early stages of this project: first, Peter Shaio, all those years ago, from Bogota; and then Ruth Petrie, in London.

I am greatly indebted to Louise Greenberg, my literary agent, who showed unremitting faith in the book.

A special mention should be made of Psyche, the parrot from Cambridge, who was the inspiration for Joacaría.

My gratitude to Antonio Dal Masetto. I used a minor character from one of his novels as the inspiration for Wanda. Also, he introduced me to a hen with a wooden leg!

Mariela, Silvana and Sebastián were my incomparable, critical fans.

Valli is, simply, the co-author of everything I write.

A Note on Translation

Fragments of the following poems and songs have been quoted in the text: "No meio do caminho", by Carlos Drummond de Andrade, from *Tentativa de Exploração do Estar-no-Mundo*, in *Antologia Poética (Organizada pelo Autor)*, 31st Edition, Rio de Janeiro/São Paulo: Editora Record, 1995; "Aquí", by Pedro Salinas, from *Razón de Amor* (1936), Buenos Aires: Editorial Losada, 1952; "fidel", by Juan Gelman, from *Gotán*, Buenos Aires: Editorial La Rosa Blindada, 1962; "Lamento per il Sud", by Salvatore Quasimodo, from *La Vita non è Sogno* (1946-1948), in *Obra Completa*, Buenos Aires: Editorial Sur, 1959; "Premièrement" (1929), by Paul Eluard, from *L'amour la poesie*, *Oeuvres Completes – Vol. 1*, Paris: Gallimard, 1968; "Lluvia", by Raúl Gonzalez Tuñón, from *Todos Bailan – Poemas de Juancito Caminador* (1934), in *La Luna con Gatillo (Selección de Poemas Líricos, Sociales y Políticos – Tomo 1)*, Buenos Aires: Editorial Cartago, 1957; "Me gustas cuando callas...", by Pablo Neruda, from *20 Poemas de Amor y una Canción Desesperada* (1924), Buenos Aires: Editorial Losada, 1944; "Babii Yar", by Serge Yevtushenko, from *No he Nacido Tarde*, Madrid: Editorial Horizonte, 1963; "Poema de sete faces", by Carlos Drummond de Andrade, from *Um Eu Todo Retorcido (Organizada pelo Autor)*, in *Antologia Poética*, 31st Edition, Rio de Janeiro/São Paulo: Editora Record, 1995; "Mi Noche Triste" (tango), lyrics by Pascual Contursi, music by Samuel Castriota, first performed by Carlos Gardel on January 3rd, 1917, at the Teatro Esmeralda; "Último poema", by Robert Desnos, from *Antología de la Poesía Surrealista de Lengua Francesa (Estudio Preliminar, Selección, Notas y Traducciones de Aldo Pellegrini)*, Barcelona/Buenos Aires: Editorial Argonauta, 1981; "Caminante...", by Antonio Machado, from *Proverbios y Cantares*, in *Campos de Castilla* (1907-1917), *Poesías Completas*, Buenos Aires: Editorial Losada, 1943; "Escuchen, mortales..." from the *Himno Nacional Argentino* (1813).

All translations and renditions were done by the author.

Printed in the United States
by Baker & Taylor Publisher Services